A NOBLE KNIGHT

A NOBLE KNIGHT

DAN PRIATKO'S
STORY OF
Faith AND *Courage*

FOREWORD BY
MIKE KRZYZEWSKI *and* DICK LEBEAU

SCOTT BROWN

XULON PRESS

God bless you with a Noble Life.

USMA 84

Xulon Press
2301 Lucien Way #415
Maitland, FL 32751
407.339.4217
www.xulonpress.com

Xulon
PRESS

Printed in the United States of America.

PAPERBACK ISBN-13: 978-1-6312-9057-2

EBOOK ISBN-13: 978-1-6312-9058-9

DEDICATION

This book is dedicated to my mother, Helen Priatko, a woman who exemplified a strong, loving, and consistent Christian faith. Even while suffering, Mom, as she had her whole life, demonstrated a sacrificial, unselfish, patient, understanding, and compassionate love toward family, friends, and all she met. Mom was strong, resolute, and persevering, all while maintaining an upbeat and positive attitude.

———- Dan Priatko

This book is dedicated to my parents, Scott and Gretchen Brown. Writing this book gave me an even greater appreciation for all that they have done for me and my sisters, Melissa and Ali, —and all they continue to do for us.

———- Scott Brown

TABLE OF CONTENTS

Acknowledgments

I t is hard to put into words how thankful and appreciative I am of everybody who helped make this a reality. I interviewed close to sixty people for the book, which is about family, faith, duty, honor, community, and, most of all, the human spirit and power of perseverance. Dan Priatko embodies all of these qualities. So does his father, Bill. This book would not have been possible without them allowing me to tell their incredible story.

That also holds true for Dan's sisters, Debbie Priatko and Kathy Sekera, and his brother, David Priatko. All three, like Dan and Bill, were generous with their time and recollections. Those recollections helped me also tell the remarkable story of Dan's mother, Helen. I never met Helen, who passed away in 2014, but after writing about her I wish I had known her. I would have been better for it. Special thanks to Duke men's basketball coach Mike Krzyzewski and former Pittsburgh Steelers defensive coordinator and Pro Football Hall of Famer Dick LeBeau for their help, and to both for writing forewords for the book. Each has a special connection to Dan and the Priatko family.

I didn't really know Dan when I started working on a story about his unique bond with Krzyzewski through West Point and the friendship that developed from there. Here is how highly college men's basketball all-time winningest coach thinks of Dan: he called me in the middle of the 2018-19 season, the day before a game no less, to do a phone interview. That is almost unheard of for a coach of that stature.

Not only did "Coach K" do that, but he never sounded hurried or impatient as we talked about Dan and Bill. I've always thought of "Coach K" as a class act, and my appreciation for him grew through this experience. The 3,000-plus words story of Dan and Coach K ran in the *Duke Basketball Report* on February 28, 2019. It received great reception but, as I told Bill, I thought it only scratched the surface of Dan's story. He and Dan allowed me to tell the rest of it in this book.

This is my ninth book, and I've been working in writing, mainly sports, for almost thirty years. I have seen and heard a lot from countless interviews yet was still surprised by some of the reactions I received. Talking about Dan reduced Joe Ravasio to tears during our phone interview. Ravasio became overcome with emotion because of the impact Dan has had on his life and how Dan has made him a better man. I honestly can't recall many reactions like that from a phone interview. Nor can I remember the end of an interview quite like the one I had with Dan Wukich. Like Ravasio, Wukich said he is better for knowing Dan, and, near the end of our phone conversation, he said, "You've got a tough job, pal." It was his way of saying that capturing the essence of Dan's with mere words might be too much. I couldn't disagree with him. I can promise Dan, the Priatko family, and everyone else who helped with this book that I did put my heart and soul into telling Dan's story. It is a story that not only deserves to be told but *needs* to be told. These are complicated, divisive, even angry times; Dan's story is an antidote to them. I truly believe that, and I again thank him and the Priatko family for allowing me to tell it.

In addition to those mentioned, thank you to those who were generous to provide interviews for the book. They include Tom Abraham, Joseph Bergantz, Nancy Bush, Kathy Camp, Hugh Campbell, Mark Critz, Nick Cutich, Philip Dahar, Kevin Donnelly, Kristy Dubinsky, Roger Fischer, Bob Flaherty, Ernie Furno, Bob "Bo" Garritano, Rick Gaudino, Andrew Glen, Nell Hartley, Charles "Ace" Heberling, Henry Heer, Don Kattic, William Kerr, Frank Klanchar, Al Lynn, Tim

McCabe, James McCague, Marcus McCullough, Rose Mologne, Joe Mucci, Bernard Murphy, Jane Murphy, Evan Offstein, Ron Peduzzi, Greg Petrick, Dimitri Petro, Art Rooney, Jr., Sam Rutigliano, Mary "Mimi" Sams, Igor Soroka, Kurtis Sekera, Mike Siyufy, Don Smith, Kate Smith, Lisa Smith, Tom Stabile, Dorothy Tragesser, Tim Tracy, Barbara Tray, John Varoscak, Dave Villiotti, Karen Watkiss, Vivian Watt, Bob Weaver, John Yaccino, and Shirley Yohman.

Thanks also to Jon Jackson, Duke University deputy athletics director/men's basketball and external affairs and Julian King, editor of *Duke Basketball Report*. Jon arranged the phone interview with Mike Krzyzewski, assisted with Coach K's foreword, and was very helpful in general. Julian helped get this book going by running the story on Dan and Krzyzewski's unique friendship on his website and I very much appreciate his help. I am also thankful to the West Point Association of Graduates for also helping initiate this project by publishing the story of Dan and Coach K's unique friendship and West Point bond on its website. Colonel Todd Browne, the president and CEO, Elizabeth Barrett, the vice president of communications and marketing, and Kim McDermott, the director of communications, provided valuable assistance.

More thanks to Bob Weaver for his drawing of Dan, Bill, and Helen that is included among the pictures in the book. Bill and I are also grateful to Cindy Henderson and Suzie Domasky of Ferrante's Lakeview in Greensburg, Pennsylvania. Bill and I met for work lunches there several times. They are always so welcoming to us— and to everyone who walks through the doors of the restaurant/banquet locale that their father, John Ferrante, built. Bill, who was close friends with John, loves to tell the story of how Bill Mazeroski enjoyed a quiet celebration at Lakeview after hitting the Game Seven home run that allowed the Pittsburgh Pirates to slay the mighty New York Yankees and win the 1960 World Series. A wall at Lakeview is adorned with photos of sports celebrities who have visited the restaurant. It is a treasure.

I would be remiss if I didn't give a hearty thank you to Mike Neilson, Gina DeHaven, and Kristen Grego at FedEx Office Print & Ship Center in Greensburg. Most of the photos in the book were scanned by Mike or scanned at FedEx with Mike, Gina, and Kristen's help. They couldn't have been nicer or more professional. The same is true of Diane Lavender and Kim Rancatore of Minuteman Press in North Versailles. Diane and Kim scanned some of the photos in the book and were very helpful. All photos in the book are courtesy of the Priatko family unless noted otherwise.

This book wouldn't have been possible without Gina Fleming, Brandye Brixius, and Marc Bermudez of Xulon Press. They were exceedingly patient and professional. Gina, Brandye, Marc, and the Xulon staff couldn't have been better stewards for this book.

Finally, we made a lot of late changes and additions. My dad, Scott, helped with the editing and did a great job. So did Bill's daughter, Kathy Sekera. Kathy is an English teacher at Penn-Trafford High School, and she was simply phenomenal. I've never worked with an editor who was as meticulous as Kathy. I can't thank her enough for the job that she did. I told Kathy that she should edit books on the side. She is that good.

——- Scott Brown

FOREWORD

D an Priatko and I share a unique bond. We are part of the Long Gray Line. To those who graduated from the United States Military Academy in West Point, N.Y., those three words mean everything. They capture shared experiences as cadets and our lifetime duty to country. Those three words also transcend time, linking all graduates of Army no matter when they came of age at West Point.

I met Dan for the first time in 1990 and, as members of the Long Gray Line, we immediately hit it off. I had learned of Dan's story through his father, Bill, and knew that a terrible car accident shortly after Dan graduated from Army Ranger School altered the Priatkos' lives forever. Dan spent almost a year in a coma and the accident left him with many challenges. It robbed him of a promising army career. What it didn't take, as I have learned over the years, was his essence, his core.

One of the things that you learn at the Academy and in the service is no excuses. Whatever situation you're placed in, you don't have an excuse for not doing something positive in that situation because no one has control over your attitude except for you. If you have the attitude to accomplish the mission, then the mission will probably be accomplished. If you have the attitude to be positive, you will stay positive.

For Dan there is no other choice except to be positive. Before his accident he had eliminated negative alternatives and excuses. Thank goodness that when he was hit with the kind of adversity that few can imagine, those things were already embedded in him and they haven't changed. They've been tested to a really high level and he has passed that test tremendously.

Dan and Bill come to a game every season at Duke and it is an honor to have them as my guests. I'll get notes from them throughout the season, and even in the offseason, keeping me up to date with what they're doing as well as encouraging or congratulating me on what I'm doing. A good friendship has developed there. You talk about solid people; Bill and Dan are at the top of the list.

Dan, with Bill, meeting Coach Mike Krzyzewski for the first time in person during Five-Star Basketball Camp at Robert Morris University in 1990.

As much as I've admired Dan's attitude toward fighting adversity and being positive, I've also admired Bill's commitment to his son because it's not a fight that you do alone. Something else really you learn at West Point is the importance of teamwork. Teams can accomplish a lot more than individuals can accomplish, and teams can overcome adversity better than one person can overcome adversity. Dan and Bill have been a real team in doing this and I truly admire that. I don't have sons, but I have daughters and I have grandchildren. I would hope that, if placed in a similar situation as Bill, I could do the job he has done. It's at the highest level.

——- Mike Krzyzewski, Duke University men's basketball coach

I didn't know it at the time, but my life changed for the better when I roomed with Bill Priatko at Cleveland Browns' training camp in 1959. We quickly became friends and stayed in touch through the years. We reconnected in 1992 when I came to Pittsburgh to coach the Steelers' defensive backs. Bill was living in North Huntingdon, a suburb of Pittsburgh, Pennsylvania, and our friendship really blossomed during the two coaching stints I enjoyed with the Steelers.

Through my friendship with Bill, I got close to his family: his wife, Helen; his daughters, Debbie and Kathy; and his sons, Dan and David, both of whom are graduates of the United States Military Academy. The highest compliment I can pay to the Priatkos is that they are an All-American family. We all go through our ups and downs, our travails, and they've certainly had theirs, but they've been able to persevere and triumph. It's all about their faith, family, and a resiliency reflected in their belief that the glass is half full. To me, these are All-American characteristics, and Dan is the epitome of those qualities.

Dan sporting one of the Super Bowl rings that Dick LeBeau won as the
Pittsburgh Steelers' defensive coordinator.

A catastrophic car accident changed the course of Dan's life, when
he was just starting it in many respects. What that accident didn't
change was who Dan is as a person. He lives by the same code that
guided him through West Point and Army Ranger School. He refused
to give up despite enormous challenges, and he has accomplished a lot
more than the medical professionals thought he would in the aftermath of his accident.

Most of us are products of our environment, whether it's our immediate family, or a coach or someone who took us under their wing, or
a teacher. They all in their own way help influence our character. Dan
had many of these influences and no one shaped him more than his
immediate family. You don't have to talk to his father and mother, sisters and brother for more than fifteen minutes to understand why Dan
is so remarkable.

From Dan's DNA and upbringing, right through his military
training, he's never taken a backward step and I don't think he ever will.
We always say, "You never give up" and "You keep fighting." These are

lessons that Dan learned not only at the Academy but through playing football at Norwin High School, where he served as a team captain his senior season, and then at West Point.

Football takes a lot of hits in today's society, but it still imparts so many life lessons. All you need to do is to examine lives like Dan Priatko's to see that they teach you never to give up and that you can get knocked down but get back up. Dan has done that, and I think he would inspire anybody through his example and incredible story.

——— Dick LeBeau, former NFL player, coach, and 2010 Pro Football Hall of Fame inductee

Chapter I

A Cruel Twist of Fate

All the way and then some.

Nothing resonated more with Dan Priatko than those six words as the rest of his life beckoned.

To many, this Army Rangers motto was just some abstract rallying cry; to Dan, it was a way of life—figuratively and then literally after completing Army Ranger School.

As winter started a steady if stubborn retreat in 1985, Dan seemed destined to do great things. The Pittsburgh-area native had graduated from the United States Military Academy, better known as Army, before completing Ranger school. Dan did not just survive the crucible that is four years at a military academy, he thrived in it. Dan graduated with high honors and as a senior, he was one of twelve battalion commanders for the 4,000-plus cadets at Army. That put Dan among the elite of the elite.

His resume wasn't all that stood out from his time at West Point. Dan looked like he had just stepped off a military recruiting poster. Closely cropped blond hair framed a taut but friendly face and accentuated his blue eyes, one of many things he inherited from his father.

Like Bill Priatko, Dan was also a people person, a nurturer. Those qualities led him back to West Point before he started the rest of his life.

Dan couldn't leave for his first deployment without saying goodbye. That didn't just mean to football coaches and favorite professors like Michael Solo, who taught Russian language and had grown to love Dan like a son, even calling him "Dan-ielle" in an accent that was thicker than a bowl of borscht. Dan also wanted to say goodbye to the West Point barber and the tailor too.

That was Dan, thinking of everyone who had helped him along the way.

Dan returned to West Point with his older sister, Debbie, in early March. His luggage was already en route to Europe, underscoring just how little time Second Lieutenant Priatko had before reporting to the United States Army Third Armored Division in Germany.

Dan and Debbie stayed with Joseph Bergantz and his wife, Helen, for a long weekend. Bergantz, a math professor and future two-star general, and Dan were devout Orthodox Christians. They had bonded at West Point over their faith and affinity for military life.

Bergantz had been a mentor to Dan. He reprised that role as Dan and Debbie got ready to drive home. The Bergantzes were worried about the weather and they tried to talk Dan and Debbie into delaying their departure for a day. It was March 4 and temperatures hovered around the mid-60s in southeastern New York.

However, lower temperatures and precipitation had been forecast in northeastern Pennsylvania, which Dan and Debbie had to drive through to get home. That area had some of the highest elevation points in the state; weather there could be decidedly unpredictable in early March.

Dan assured his hosts he would be careful. He and Debbie promised to call when they got home.

Right after they exchanged goodbyes, Dan slid into the driver's seat and said to Debbie, "Put your seatbelt on."

It was more an order than a reminder. Dan also told his sister that he didn't care if Pennsylvania did not yet require the use of seatbelts in moving cars. She was keeping her seatbelt on for the entire trip.

Debbie didn't argue.

The Priatkos seemed straight out of central casting for some idealized TV family of the 1950s. Only there was nothing scripted or fictional about them.

Bill, a former NFL player who had played for his hometown Steelers, was a strong father figure who always put his family first. He once passed on a big promotion at the Volkswagen plant where he worked because it would have required him to work nights and miss seeing his kids' games and other activities. Given the ultimatum of taking the job or finding work elsewhere, he chose his family. Bill worked three jobs to put food on the table and keep clothes on his children's backs. He spent several years substitute teaching for $11,000 a year. He supplemented that meager salary by working nights and weekends as a security guard or loading trucks at a local warehouse.

Helen held the family together as much as her husband did during those trying times. She was always home when the kids returned from school but also cleaned houses to earn extra money, despite her husband's objections.

The foundation that Bill and Helen provided showed in their four children. They were hard-working, respectful, polite, and as God-fearing as their parents.

Like all children, they dabbled in the occasional mischief. One time, Dan got angry with his younger brother, David, and threw a football at him. The ill-fated throw broke a window. Dan felt so bad about the incident he wrote Bill and Helen a letter of contrition in block letters.

DEAR MOM AND DAD,

I BROKE THE BOTTOM WINDOW ON THE FRONT DOOR. I WAS MAD AT DAVID. I

THREW THE FOOTBALL AT HIM. I MISSED. IT
HIT THE WINDOW AND IT BROKE. I KNOW
I SHOULDN'T HAVE DONE IT. I KNOW THE
WINDOW COST MONEY. PLEASE FORGIVE
ME. I AM VERY SORRY.

LOVE,
DAN

Debbie, Dan, David, and Kathy varied in ages and interests, but the Priatko children bonded over many things. Near the top of the list were the Steelers and Helen's famous treats—she always told them "You'll find out after dinner" when they excitedly asked her what was for dessert. Dan and Debbie were lucky enough to be included on a motorhome trip to Pittsburgh's 1974 Super Bowl appearance, the first in franchise history. As extended members of the Priatko family rode to New Orleans, Debbie, Dan and a couple of their cousins collaborated on a song that they sang to the tune of *Oh! Susanna.*

Oh, we came to New Orleans today
To clap and yell and cheer
The big one we will win today
Because it is our year
Super Steelers, the Vikes will tumble down
And proudly we'll be number one
As we ride out of town

That kind of wholesome fun defined the Priatkos, and the children thrived in a home that stressed structure but also brimmed with love. The Priatkos were not wealthy but they were rich by most measures. Bill and Helen enjoyed a storybook marriage, and they raised four happy, healthy, and dutiful children amidst a backdrop of suburban bliss.

Everything changed on March 4, 1985.

The day had been unremarkable for Bill and Helen except for the weather. It was unseasonably warm in North Huntingdon Township, a bedroom community twenty miles east of Pittsburgh. Temperatures climbed as high as 65 degrees during the day, something that should have put the normally upbeat Bill into an even better mood. But, as he and Helen sat down to dinner, something felt off and Bill couldn't figure out why. Finally, he said to Helen, "What's the matter with me? Why do I feel so sad?"

A couple of minutes later the phone rang. It was Debbie.

"Dad, Dan and I have been in an accident," she said in a hushed voice from Hazleton Hospital. "The state trooper said he's fighting for his life."

I t might not have been manifest destiny for Dan to end up in the military, but it was pretty darn close. And it can be traced to Grant Street in North Braddock, Pennsylvania.

Bill grew up in the steel mill town just outside of Pittsburgh, and the outbreak of World War II revealed the ties that bound his world together. Young men from the five streets that comprised First Ward in North Braddock enlisted to fight with the fate of the free world hanging in the balance. Their pictures were taped inside a front window of their respective houses, and everyone in the neighborhood knew who they were and in which theater they were fighting. They also knew to pray for those young men every night.

One day in 1944, the basketball court on Grant Street teemed with young boys. It was the championship game in an annual tournament among First Ward's five streets and it pitted Grant Street, Bill's team, against Grandview Avenue. Bragging rights meant everything to these young boys and the title game, which had a heathy audience, was hotly contested.

The game stopped when a car pulled up in front of Mary Korbel's house across the street. Frankie Korbel, who lived two houses down from Bill, had enlisted in the Marines and was fighting in the Pacific. He was the only son of Mary Korbel and the man of the house since his father had died years earlier.

A Marine dressed in full uniform stepped out of the car, turning the boys' curiosity into sickening horror. They knew before Mrs. Korbel that Frankie had been killed in action. And they were close enough to hear Mrs. Korbel after she received the news.

"Oh, my dear God!" she wailed. "No! No! Not my Frankie! No!"

The boys watched with tears in their eyes, and the game ended right there. Suddenly, being the champion of First Ward wasn't so important after all. Bill, standing on the asphalt court that had been his world moments earlier, vowed that he would one day serve his country in memory of Frankie Korbel.

Fast forward to that same street in 1950.

Bill was sitting on a curb with Paul Olson, whom he looked up to as a big brother. Olson had fought against the Nazis in Italy and later in the Battle of the Bulge, an Allied victory that led to the surrender of Germany. He had also been a close friend of Frankie Korbel. Olson stayed in the army after World War II and by 1950, he faced a big decision. He could reenlist or return home and take a job in the Braddock Post Office. The decision seemed like an easy one.

Tension between the United States and Soviet Union had mounted before the end of World War II, and competing ideologies threatened to collide in Korea. The small country had been divided into two after the war with communist North Korea and South Korea separated only by a thin demilitarized zone.

War seemed inevitable while Olson was home on leave. Six of his friends were on the curb with him and Bill, then a freshman at the

University of Pittsburgh. They tried to talk him into coming home for good. With his combat experience, they told him, he would end up on the front lines if war erupted in Korea.

"If that happens, I'm a soldier," Olson said that day. "I'd go."

Olson reenlisted mere months before North Korea invaded South Korea. The North Koreans quickly overran the South Koreans, nearly pushing their troops into the Pacific Ocean. Olson was among the first American troops sent to South Korea to blunt the siege. He was killed his first week there, his platoon overwhelmed despite a valiant stand.

Olson, who was twenty-nine at the time of his death, was buried near a Methodist church on Grandview Avenue. Pallbearers carried his casket from the church to his final resting place. All were fellow World War II veterans, including Bill's older brother, John. Not once during the mile trek to the cemetery did the six men put down the casket.

After the service, the Olson family gave the American flag that had been draped on the casket to Bill. He never forgot that.

Bill went to Pitt on a football scholarship but also joined the Air Force ROTC. He graduated as a second lieutenant and was stationed at Bolling Air Force Base in Washington, D.C. Bill served in the Honor Guard, which ceremoniously greeted President Dwight D. Eisenhower and visiting dignitaries at Washington National Airport. He also participated in military funerals at Arlington Cemetery. Every funeral there made him think of Frankie Korbel.

Bill passed the ideal of serving his country to his sons, and Dan took a real interest in the Air Force Academy when he was in junior high school. It wasn't fleeting. Nor was the commitment needed to get into one of the country's military academies.

Dan excelled in his studies and served as both class president and captain of the football team as a senior at Norwin High School. He was named the school's Most Outstanding Male Student and his football coaches and teammates voted him Norwin's Most Valuable Player.

He received appointments to the Air Force Academy and Army. All things being equal, Dan probably would have gone to Air Force. However, his eyesight wasn't good enough to become a fighter pilot or even a navigator. Thus, he turned his attention to Army.

Everything seemed to line up when Bill and Dan visited Army in March 1980, a couple of months before he graduated from Norwin. On the drive to West Point, they saw signs for Promised Land, a Pennsylvania state park, and Lords Valley, a tiny hamlet in the northeastern part of the state. The signs did not go unnoticed.

"Are these bolstering my prayers that I should go to West Point?" Dan asked Bill.

Cadets marching on The Plain is one of the most spectacular and iconic sights at West Point. Photo courtesy of United States Military Academy.

The two, like most who visit West Point, were mesmerized by its majesty and aura. Before leaving, Dan and Bill drove to a hill that overlooks the academy. Dan got out of the car and drank in the breathtaking view. Looking at something so steeped in history, he saw his future.

He returned to the car and told Bill, "I will be back. I'm going to West Point."

That proclamation wasn't all that made the trip to New York so memorable. Dan and Bill had laughed and laughed after passing a sign on Route 81 for the hometown of Hometown. They joked about someone from there getting asked what was his or her hometown and saying, "Hometown." They imagined the hilarity that might ensue, something straight out of Abbot and Costello's famed act, "Who's on First?"

"We will never forget the name of Hometown," Bill said to Dan with a laugh.

Less than six months later, Dan found himself at West Point. It was no joking matter. He was surrounded by cadets who had also been class presidents, captains of their respective sports teams, and winners of their school's most outstanding student awards.

But Dan never wavered at West Point, even during his trying first year as a plebe. He never thought of quitting either when he could have drowned during Army Airborne School after an errant drop in a Florida swamp or during Army Ranger School when frostbite almost cost him a couple of toes. Graduating from Ranger school before his first deployment seemed to be one more rung on a ladder that might lead Dan to exalted status one day.

That climb came to an abrupt and tragic halt on March 4.

Plummeting temperatures and precipitation turned Route 81 around Hazleton, Pennsylvania, into a treacherous stretch of ice-covered highway. According to the *Pottsville Republican*, there were twenty-two car accidents on Route 81 during a six-hour period. The most serious of those accidents involved Dan and Debbie.

Dan lost control of his two-door Oldsmobile Cutlass Sierra Supreme. It slammed into an underpass on the driver's side of the car.

Until that point, Dan seemed to have everything going for him. Now, two weeks before his 23rd birthday, he was fighting for his life.

D an gave Bill and Helen a scare when he was just three years old. One day he came down with heavy chest congestion. Young Dan struggled to breathe as Bill frantically drove Helen and him to the hospital. There, Dan was placed in an oxygen tent; Bill and Helen could only watch helplessly and pray. Steam was pumped into the small tent as tears rolled down young Dan's face. Neither Bill nor Helen ever forgot the emotional exhaustion they experienced that day.

Years later, they dealt with something much worse with their youngest daughter, Kathy. She was just nine months old when she came down with a fever of 107 degrees the night before Valentine's Day. When Bill got home from work, Helen told him to call an ambulance. A crew got there quickly and transported Kathy to nearby Jeannette Hospital. Dr. Martin Murcek, who had gone to Pitt with Bill, met them there.

When Murcek came out of the Intensive Care Unit, Bill said, "Doc, it's good to see you but not here under these conditions."

Bill wasn't prepared for what he heard next. Murcek told them Kathy had a deadly bronchial infection and that he had done everything he could.

"There's no hope," he said gently.

Murcek had considered life-flighting Kathy to Children's Hospital in Pittsburgh but she wasn't strong enough to survive the trip. Kathy remained in the ICU and her hospital chart was marked "moribund." That was code for imminent death.

Helen's brother, an Assembly of God minister, and Father Igor Soroka from the Priatkos' Orthodox church in Donora arrived at the hospital around ten o'clock. They prayed for Kathy with Bill and Helen. Afterward, Bill took an emotionally exhausted Helen home to get some rest.

He returned to the hospital and spent the night there hoping against hope. The next morning, at around eight o'clock, an anesthesiologist ran down the hallway shouting, "Martin! Martin! I can't believe it! That little girl is breathing on her own!"

Bill sprang out of his seat. Murcek smiled broadly when Bill found him. Kathy was indeed breathing on her own.

"Dr. Murcek," Bill said, "I don't know how to thank you."

"Bill, don't thank me," Murcek said. "The good Lord must have plans for her."

That higher powers were at work with Kathy gained more credence after Bill returned home to give Helen and the other children the good news. Helen told him about a dream she had the previous night. She had been standing in the kitchen and looking at the backyard. There was a light, she told Bill, and someone in a green robe. She couldn't see the face but told Bill that the person's hands were raised. She heard a voice say, "Rise. Rise."

That confirmed to Bill and Helen that Kathy's recovery had been nothing short of miraculous.

Now, they needed another miracle after receiving Debbie's phone call from Hazleton Hospital.

The impact of the collision ripped the top of the car from the windshield. The steering wheel had been jerked violently to the left, ending up next to the driver side door. Dan suffered a traumatic brain injury, a punctured lung, and broken pelvis bone. The crash also folded his diaphragm like an accordion. Debbie suffered injuries in the accident too, including broken ribs, but fortunately none were life-threatening.

Bill and Helen didn't know any of these details, or that Dan had slipped into a coma, as they quickly threw some clothes into a suitcase for the drive to Hazleton. They said a prayer before leaving with Bill holding his mother's Bible and asking Jesus Christ to give them peace.

Each felt unusually calm during the long drive despite not knowing what awaited them. When they got close to Hazleton, fog had become so thick that Bill took an exit off Route 81. He wanted to see if a short break would give the weather time to move through the area. He pulled into a parking lot of a restaurant that was closed for the night. Its sign was still lit and Bill almost did a double take.

They were at Napoli's Pizza Place. It was the same restaurant where Bill and Dan had stopped for dinner on their way to visit West Point almost to the day five years earlier.

When Bill later looked back on the accident, he couldn't help but wistfully shake his head at some of the eerie coincidences that surrounded it. Dan's demolished car had been towed to nearby Hometown. That was the name that had given Bill and Dan such laughs when they first visited West Point. A nurse at Hazleton Hospital gave Bill a pair of blood-stained blue jeans that Dan had been wearing. He rummaged through the pockets to recover Dan's wallet or anything else of value. He found a bunch of nickels, dimes, and quarters. They totaled $3.19, the month and day of Dan's birthday.

That Dan's accident happened near Hazleton also had some significance. His high school coach, John Yaccino, hailed from there. The award Dan received at West Point as a senior for having the highest grade-point average among Army football players was named in memory of Major William Whitehead, Jr., a Hazleton native and West Point football player killed in Vietnam.

If such coincidences were a little unnerving, the cosmic forces that lined up against Dan on that fateful day seemed positively unfair—if not diabolical. Dan had almost always done the right thing. Yet everything went wrong for him on March 4.

As soon as they encountered bad weather, Dan turned on the car headlights and windshield wipers and drove well under the speed limit. He lost control of his car on a rare stretch of highway in which there were no guardrails. Had Dan's accident happened just about anywhere else on I-81 he probably would have walked away from the accident.

The road conditions and a spate of car accidents that night prevented paramedics from reaching Dan and Debbie quickly. Even after they got to Dan and Debbie, it took them forty-five minutes to cut Dan out of the car. The hospital Dan was rushed to was not nearly as equipped to deal with traumatic brain injuries as hospitals in bigger cities.

SERIOUSLY INJURED — Shown above is the car in which Daniel A. Priatko, 22, and his wife Debbie, 24, of North Huntingdon Pa., were seriously injured when the car skidded on the southbound lanes of Interstate 81 near Delano yesterday afternoon and struck a concrete bridge abutment. Shown with the auto is Joseph Gavana, chief of the West End Rescue Co. of Mahanoy City. Personnel from the rescue squad worked for 45 minutes with the "Jaws of Life" to free

This picture of Dan's car after the accident was published in a Hazleton, Pa.- area newspaper.

Simple timing produced the biggest what-if.

Dan and Debbie had moved back their trip a day after Dan received a request from General Willard Scott, the superintendent of West Point. Scott was going to be in Pittsburgh for an Army event. He requested that Dan drive him the day he was there. Dan was flattered and never considered declining the request. Had Dan and Debbie made the trip as originally planned they would have been driving home a day earlier.

Bill and Helen didn't have time to ponder any of that after arriving at Hazleton Hospital and receiving a dire prognosis.

Doctors didn't expect Dan to survive. Even if Dan pulled through, doctors told Bill and Helen, he probably wouldn't be able to walk, talk, or feed himself again. Whether in denial or falling back on their unshakable faith, Bill and Helen refused to believe that Dan wouldn't make anything but a full recovery.

They quickly learned they would not face the struggle alone.

More than 4,000 West Point cadets stood at breakfast and said a prayer for Dan the day after his accident. Father Igor Soroka of St. Nicholas Orthodox Church in Donora drove fourteen hours round trip just so he could pray for Dan in person.

Bill was just as touched when three laypeople also made the long drive to support him.

Bill Abraham and twin brothers Ron and Rey Peduzzi all had close ties to the Priatkos. Ron was the principal at Norwin and Rey was the principal at neighboring Penn-Trafford High School. Abraham was a longtime family friend and football coach at Hempfield High School. When Bill saw them in the hospital lobby, he fought back tears.

"A Hempfield Spartan, a Norwin Knight, and a Penn-Trafford Warrior," he told them. "You guys are something."

Such visits were steady though sometimes Bill had to do the consoling. His older brother, John, was Dan's godfather and, typical of so many of his generation, a World War II veteran and a tough guy. But even what he had experienced in battle couldn't prepare him for the sight of Dan lying in a hospital bed with tubes crisscrossing his body.

He broke down sobbing.

Michael Solo, Dan's Russian language professor at West Point, did the same thing when he talked to Bill. Dan and Solo had developed a special bond at West Point. One day in class Dan fell asleep. He had stayed up all night studying but that couldn't be used as an excuse. And sleeping in class at West Point was different than at most other schools. It was a dereliction of duty, punishable by eight demerits and four hours of solitary marching.

"Mr. Priatko, I know you tink you know everytink there is to know about Russian," Solo said in his Russian accent and sometimes broken English. "But!!!"

The last word jolted Dan awake. Solo did not report Dan for the transgression, cutting him a rare break because of how much he had grown to like Dan and respect him as a student. News of Dan's accident jolted Solo four years later. It broke his heart and his grief poured through the phone when Bill talked to him.

"No! No! Mine dear Jesus Christ! No," he wailed.

Solo died two weeks later from a massive heart attack – and possibly a broken heart. He had been that hurt by what had happened to Dan.

During Dan's stay at Hazleton Hospital, Army football coach Jim Young's voice was a constant in his room. A couple of Dan's Army football teammates visited Dan and dropped off a tape recording that Young had made.

"Dan, remember when I used to tell you guys in the locker room that what the mind can conceive, the body can achieve," Young said. "Remember that Dan. You'll make it."

That was one of Young's favorite sayings, and Bill and Helen were convinced that Dan could hear it even though he was in a coma. They played the tape over and over for him.

Support from western Pennsylvania and West Point, like Young's tape, seemed to run on an endless loop for the Priatkos.

Then two people came into their lives when they needed it most.

Rev. Bernard Murphy walked into the ICU waiting room a week into Dan's stay at Hazleton Hospital. He pointed at Bill and said something Bill never expected to hear so far from home.

"I'm a Norwin Knight," Murphy said. "Your Dan's a Norwin Knight."

Bill wasn't sure what to make of the introduction, but Murphy quickly filled him in. He too had graduated from Norwin High School and had heard from Bill Snyder.

Snyder owned a funeral home in Irwin, Pennsylvania, and had grown up with Murphy. Snyder and Bill were good friends through a men's fellowship group in Irwin. Snyder called Murphy shortly after Dan's accident and told him about the tragic turn of events.

Murphy promised Snyder that he would visit Dan and the Priatkos in the hospital.

One visit turned into another, and before long he was stopping by the hospital daily. One day Murphy told Bill and Helen that he and his wife, Jane, had a four-bedroom house with three open rooms. He insisted the Priatkos stay with them, and their offer couldn't have come at a better time. Bill and Helen's money had been stretched thin by the daily expense of lodging. Plus, the Murphys lived just three blocks from the hospital.

The arrangement proved to be much more than cost-effective and convenient. The Murphys became a constant presence in Bill and Helen's lives during this most precarious time. Jane scrambled eggs or made pancakes and served them with bacon every morning. Bill and Helen returned home from long days at the hospital and prayed with Bernard and Jane at the same kitchen table where they had eaten breakfast.

Their first Sunday with the Murphys, Bill and Helen attended their Methodist church. They received a standing ovation from the congregation and the hymn "Because He Lives I Can Face Tomorrow" had been picked for Bill and Helen. It became a staple of services while the Priatkos stayed in Hazleton.

Despite such support, Bill and Helen started to wear down physically and emotionally. Dan remained in a coma, and a couple of weeks after the accident, they started to question whether everything would work out. Maybe their fatigue was inevitable. Interminable days at the hospital and the constant worrying had ground them down.

They were figurative nubs one night when they retired to their bedroom after praying with the Murphys. They were about to kneel at their bedside for more prayer when they heard a loud bang accompanied by blinding light. It was like a cannon had been fired at the same time as a thousand bulbs flashed.

Bill and Helen jumped up. Bill looked out the window, one that offered a full view of the nearby church parking lot. It was perfectly still outside. It didn't make any sense, and Bill took it as a sign.

"Lord," he said, "You're giving us a message."

He grabbed the Bible sitting on a bedside table. He closed his eyes and told Helen that wherever his finger ended up would reveal the message God had sent them. Bill's right index finger landed on Hebrews 10:23 and the passage that reads, "Hold fast, the profession of your faith without wavering, for He is faithful who promised."

God was telling them to hang in there. Energy coursed through Bill's body. He told Helen how much stronger he suddenly felt.

"I feel the same way," she said.

The next morning Jane asked the question before Bill or Helen could pose it: "What was the explosion last night?" Bill and Helen told the Murphys the story and how they couldn't explain it. They said it had been a revelation, one they needed in the worst way.

"Yes," Bernard said, nodding. "Yes."

"And from that moment on," Bill said years later, "we never lost faith."

Not everyone shared that faith.

Helen got a stark reminder of that while Dan was getting transferred to Walter Reed National Military Medical Center outside of Washington, D.C. As Dan was wheeled to the ambulance that would take him to nearby Wilkes-Barre/Scranton Airport, a nurse gave Helen a plastic bag with several locks of blond hair in it. She had saved the hair, after Dan's head had been shaved so the doctors could insert a brain monitoring device.

The nurse told Helen, "You might need this for the viewing."

Helen didn't scold the nurse. Didn't even glare at her. She simply smiled.

"No," Helen said, "we won't need that."

Dan inherited many things from his father. Size wasn't one of them. Bill was six-foot, one inch, with broad shoulders, hands that gripped like a vise, and seemingly superhuman strength. Bill faithfully lifted weights growing up, at a time when it was neither advanced nor widely embraced. That and a strong work ethic helped shape him into a player who starred at Pitt and spent time in the NFL before a serious leg injury prematurely ended his football career.

Dan got his size from his mother, Helen. He topped out at five-foot, nine inches and played football at less than 150 pounds early in his Norwin High School career. He never let his size define him on the football field—or anywhere else.

Dan joined his junior high track team one year with the goal of becoming a hurdler. Short legs and less than blazing speed would have discouraged most from this endeavor. But where others saw insurmountable obstacles—perhaps literally in this case—Dan saw challenges that could be overcome through sheer determination.

That ethos explained why he sometimes drew a crowd at practice. Dan would often clear the first couple of hurdles but get his leg caught on the next one. That sent Dan sprawling and left him face down on the cinder track. His teammates watched and laughed, not to poke fun at Dan, but because they knew he wouldn't give up no matter how many times he fell.

"He probably still has half of the track's cinders in his knees," said Greg Petrick, Dan's classmate and teammate at Norwin.

"He was determined to be a hurdler," added Kevin Donnelly, another classmate and teammate of Dan's. "I think the coaches finally told him, 'Dan, you might want to be doing something else. You're tearing up our equipment and you're tearing up our track.'"

His short-lived hurdling days represented one of the few times that Dan didn't succeed. But more instructive, and why he *did* so often succeed, was his response to falling. He just kept getting up.

"He didn't know defeat," Donnelly said. "That's the only way I can describe him. He just knew situations and ways to overcome something."

Dan took that mentality into the fight of his life. The fight *for* his life.

When Dan arrived at Walter Reed Military Medical Center on March 29, he was still unresponsive, breathing through a tube and taking his meals through IV lines.

The car accident probably should have killed him. Even if he came out of the coma, doctors didn't know what kind of life he would have. He would probably never walk or talk again. Even the most optimistic doctors would have concluded this.

But there are things that don't register on CAT scans and MRIs and can't be accounted for within the confines of medicine. The most significant one of those, as Dan lay in a coma, was Dan himself.

And his indomitable will.

Chapter II

A Born Leader

D aniel Andrew Priatko was born March 19, 1962, the first son
and second child of Bill and Helen Priatko. His middle name
was in honor of the paternal grandfather he never met.

Dan arrived two weeks after Bill and Helen moved to North
Huntingdon, outside of Pittsburgh. They fashioned their own slice
of suburbia on a two-acre plot about a mile from Route 30. The split-
level house, constructed from white brick, has four bedrooms, and Bill
and Helen filled the home with four kids: Debbie, Dan, David, and
Kathy. The two boys shared a bedroom and spent just as much time
together in a spacious backyard that eventually turned into a hub for
neighborhood kids.

Born almost two years after Debbie, Dan was an easy baby. He
rarely fussed and always seemed so happy. He wiggled his fingers when
he got excited and rarely gave Bill and Helen any problems except for
refusing to eat peas and mushrooms — and occasionally interrupting
their sleep.

One time, when Dan was three years old, he padded into his parents'
bedroom in the middle of the night. He woke them up so he could tell
Helen that she was a "good cooker." The sentiment was sweet, though

Dan could have waited until morning to compliment his mother. Alas, toddlers aren't any better at timing than they are trigonometry.

Dan and Debbie always seemed to be smiling as young children.

Bill and Helen raised their children to be responsible, respectful, kind, and hard-working. They were also determined to give their children a foundation beyond what they received at home. After moving to North Huntingdon, Bill and Helen conducted a thorough search for a church. They found one they loved in Donora and didn't mind that St. Nicholas Orthodox Church was an hour away. They felt comfortable with Father Igor Soroka, who would become an institution at St Nicholas and a big part of their family.

The kids were expected to do their best in school but also enjoy their youth. Kids from all over could usually find a game of football, kickball, dodgeball, Wiffle ball; any sport really that lent itself to a grassy expanse in the Priatko backyard. Bill and Helen loved hearing the laughter and occasional arguments among the children, and there were only two rules: no cursing or playing in the yard in early March when it was muddy. Dan, David, and their friends ignored this rule one time and tore up the yard. They lucked out when a storm covered the yard with snow for two weeks. It was all part of growing up at that time amidst bordering neighborhoods filled with kids.

"I wouldn't trade those experiences for anything," Dan said.

The one quintessential boyhood experience that Dan didn't enjoy was Little League baseball. After a couple of practices, he no longer wanted to play. Bill allowed him to stop after Dan said he didn't think the game was for him. It may be the one documented time that Dan Priatko quit something, though it could be framed as an early retirement.

Dan loved football, taking after his father. He played it in all pick-up variations until Bill allowed Dan to play organized football in junior high school. Dan prepared for upcoming seasons with his own version of minicamp for himself and any friends who dared to join him. They gathered in the Priatko backyard, putting themselves through drills that included bear crawls, forward and backward sprints, and Carioca drills, which are lateral slides that improve footwork and agility. Nothing thrilled Dan and his friends more than when next-door neighbor Hank Yohman, a star tight end at Norwin High School, stopped over to give them pointers. The younger kids would huddle around him, as if he were Mike Ditka or Dave Casper, and hang on his every word.

Dan's youth was so normal that it almost seems cliché. He had paper routes and cut grass to earn spending money. He went to church every Sunday and played sports with his friends. If Dan consistently defied his parents, it was when they told him lights out at night. Sometimes he snuck into his closet and turned on the light there so he could continue reading. That qualified as the trouble that Dan caused in the home.

A Priatko family Christmas (Debbie, Dan, David, and Kathy in back and Bill and Helen in front)

"He had my mother's personality," Debbie said. "Never yelled, was never harsh. He was sweet."

Dan may have been sweet, but he also had a fierce desire to succeed. His three years at Norwin High School proved that these two things did not have to be mutually exclusive.

The Norwin Knights football team had an annual ritual under coach John Yaccino. Players and coaches piled into buses in August and rode to the Pocono Mountains in northeast Pennsylvania. They spent a week of preseason practice there. Yaccino, who coached Norwin from 1974-80, hailed from that part of the state, and he liked the trips for several reasons. It broke up the monotony of preseason practice, helped with team bonding and limited distractions for his players.

One night, Rick Gaudino heard a thump in the cabin he was sharing with Dan and a handful of other players. He grabbed a flashlight and shined it around the room. He found the source of the noise when the light settled on Dan.

He was on the floor doing push-ups in the dark.

"What sixteen- or seventeen-year-old kid does that?" Gaudino said with a laugh.

Such dedication was normal for Dan, even at the Poconos where Yaccino put his players through as many as *four* practices a day.

During the summer, Dan ran most mornings at Norwin High School with his cousin, Hugh Campbell. Campbell was a year older than Dan and had longer legs. Despite these advantages, he found it pointless to tell Dan he didn't have to keep pace with him, especially during the diabolical stretch that ended their runs. It was a steep incline and felt more like climbing a ladder than running a hill. The final kick often left Campbell dizzy and gasping for breath.

And Dan?

"He ran so hard that he would throw up half the time," Campbell said.

Dan needed to push himself to extremes to keep up with players like Campbell, a standout guard who later earned a full scholarship to Maine University. He was not blessed with size. Nor did he possess one of the most important qualities for a running back.

"I didn't have great speed," Dan said. "My father always told me, 'Hit the hole quick.'"

He had some success in junior high, but one of his teammates had doubts whether Dan could play for a high school with such a large enrollment like Norwin.

"He was slow as molasses," Mark Critz said with a laugh. "If you had asked me in eighth grade if Dan was going to do anything football-wise I would have said, 'He's certainly determined.' But you start going up in levels and the competition starts getting extremely difficult. He worked at it and worked at it and worked at it."

It paid off his first year in high school when Dan was among the handful of sophomores picked by the coaches to go away for preseason practice in the Poconos.

That season he played running back on the scout team, helping to prepare a first-team defense that featured several future Division I players for upcoming opponents. Playing scout-team running back is as thankless a job as there is in football. But Dan, all five-feet-nine and 145 pounds of him, never flinched amidst the daily punishment.

"They just beat the crap out of us, but Danny was so tough," said Bob Flaherty, who was the scout-team quarterback. "I was so out of breath I could barely call the plays. He never said a word."

Dan's resolve won him the respect of his teammates.

"Danny was on the small side, but he always gave everything he had," said Gaudino, who was a year ahead of Dan and played linebacker and guard. "Too bad Dan didn't have size because who knows what would have happened."

Dan played well enough to letter as a junior and start at running back his senior season. To the surprise of no one, he also served as one of the team captains.

"He was just one of those special kids," said Ernie Furno, who played wide receiver, safety, and punter and was also a captain with Dan. "Always the first one to practice. Always making sure we were in the weight room."

Dan's innate drive made him one of the more unique players that Yaccino coached during his well-traveled career, which spanned four decades.

"He was probably one of the most determined kids that I've had," Yaccino said. "Once he put his mind to doing something, even though his abilities might have limited him, he would end up getting it done. Whenever he was told he had to block someone, I could almost see him doing it. I think that's the way he pursued anything in his life. Very determined. Never gave up."

One of the biggest highlights of Dan's career came in the second game of his junior season. It showed his mettle even if it came in an unlikely situation.

Trailing Latrobe, 6-0, Norwin scored a touchdown on game's last play. Norwin's starting kicker had pulled a muscle earlier in the game, but no one beyond Norwin's sidelines knew it because the Knights hadn't needed him after the opening kickoff. Yaccino could go for the 2-point conversion or try to win the game with his backup kicker.

"Priatko, go in there and kick it!" he barked.

Bill was stunned to see Dan trotting onto the field for the first kick of his varsity career. Maybe he shouldn't have been worried. Dan, like most other times, was prepared for the moment. He had spent hours kicking in the Priatko backyard growing up, often enlisting David and sometimes even Kathy to shag balls for him.

Dan's kick easily cleared the outstretched hands of Latrobe defenders trying to block it. It split the uprights, unleashing pandemonium on the Norwin sidelines.

L ike the kick that made him a hero, everything seemed to go smoothly for Dan in high school.

Dan excelled in the classroom and was named Outstanding Male Student of his senior class. That year his peers voted him class president and Polka King. The latter, awarded at a school dance, may not have meant much for posterity, but it was another indication of how well-liked Dan was at Norwin. And not just by his classmates.

"He was very conscientious, very sincere, very polite and just very much of a gentleman, even as a young man," said Vivian Watt, an English teacher who was the class advisor when Dan was president. "I could just go on and on with every positive adjective that you could think of and that would describe Dan."

Ultra-achievers who are beloved by teachers often engender resentment among at least a portion of their classmates. Not Dan.

"There was never one person who had a bad word to say about him," Bob Flaherty said. "He wasn't boastful. He wasn't arrogant. His humility was a big reason why he was so loved."

Dan's senior class picture at Norwin High School

Dan appealed to everybody because he didn't belong to one group and couldn't be stereotyped. He was the captain of the football team who also sang in the school chorus. He did his thing and never looked down on or judged anyone who did their thing.

"Dan was always sure of who he was, and at that age you don't always see that," said Nancy Bush (Hensler), who starred on Norwin's girls' volleyball team. "Across the board he had respect from all the kids. They just kind of knew who he was and that was his place in the whole class. Nobody thought of him as uncool or anything like that."

Indeed, Dan may have been straight as a blade of grass, but he also flashed a mischievous streak that could test the patience of teachers. It surfaced early in his academic career, something that led to a meeting between his backside and a wooden paddle.

When Dan was in fifth grade, a teacher got exasperated with him for goofing around a little bit. He yelled at Dan and said, "What are you, the class clown?"

Dan whispered to a classmate, "How much pay do I get?"

The classmate started laughing and then fessed up what Dan had said when the teacher asked what was so funny.

That earned Dan a paddling but didn't quell his sense of humor.

That Dan had a less serious side probably helped make him popular with his classmates. He was not a robot, driven as he was, and showed a quick wit and sense of humor.

One summer, Bill drove Helen and the kids to Colorado for two weeks of Air Force Reserves service. He plotted the course so the Priatkos could visit as many football stadiums as possible. One of those stops was at hallowed Notre Dame Stadium in South Bend, Indiana. Bill had played there in 1952, helping Pitt upset eighth-ranked Notre Dame, 22-19.

They stopped in the football offices so Bill could visit Notre Dame coach Dan Devine and use the bathroom. Bill started looking at a glass display with pictures of Notre Dame's Heisman Trophy winners and noticed one missing: Johnny Lattner, winner of the 1953 Heisman Trophy. He pointed out the oversight to Notre Dame athletics director Moose Krause.

The two were talking when Dan came running out of the bathroom. "Dad! Dad! You won't believe it!" he said. "When you flush the toilet, it plays the Notre Dame fight song!" Dan seemed so genuinely excited that Bill almost believed him. Krause started laughing.

"You know what?" he said. "That's a pretty good idea. I might implement that."

Krause was kidding too, depriving Dan of leaving his mark at Notre Dame. No matter. He left plenty of one at Norwin.

After receiving appointments to two military academies, Dan fell in love with Army and accepted its appointment. No one doubted he would succeed there.

"Dan learned to become a leader early, and it carried him through to West Point," said Karen Watkiss, a longtime secretary at Norwin. "He was just what you think all your students should be like."

When asked if his job as a principal would have been easier had all his students been like Dan, Ron Peduzzi laughed. Then he paid Dan the ultimate compliment.

"He probably is the top student that (ever) graduated from Norwin Senior High School," said Peduzzi, a teacher and principal at Norwin for more than forty years. "You didn't have to discipline him, and he was very serious and conscientious about everything he did. He was a leader."

I t would make a good chicken or the egg question: Was Dan destined for the military because he was such a leader or did the military's gravitational pull help mold Dan into a good leader?

Whatever the case there is no question that Dan—and his younger brother David—were infatuated with the military at an early age. They loved when Bill returned home from Air Force Reserves duty wearing his flight uniform and garrison cap. Dan would wear the oversized cap and parade around the house. Bill named him "Captain Dan."

Bill passed on to his sons the patriotism that had been imbued in him at a young age. Dan and David didn't consider their shared duty of raising the American flag every morning in the front yard a chore. They were more likely to argue over who got to do it rather than who had to do it.

Dan's favorite teacher at Norwin was John Polivka. On the first day of school the history teacher told his students, "We're on a ship. USS Respect." He demanded respect for learning and respect for his students' fellow classmates. Polivka even insisted that all the desks be lined up in an orderly way. Dan loved it.

"He set the environment if you wanted to learn," Dan said.

Dan and Greg Petrick pushed each other as much as any of their teachers did. The two classmates became best friends and friendly rivals. Each received an appointment to the Air Force Academy, something they had talked about since junior high school. Petrick happily accepted but it wasn't as simple for Dan. He wanted to fly fighter planes but did not have the required vision for a pilot or even navigator.

That didn't rule out Air Force, but it did get him thinking about Army. But he had an issue there too.

Dan needed a nomination from Congressman Don Bailey. The U.S. Representative was more than happy to oblige but he had already used his nominations for the year. He successfully petitioned Vice President Walter Mondale to nominate Dan, and Dan was accepted to Army.

That left Bill with what he feared might be an awkward conversation. Pitt athletic director Casimir "Cas" Myslinski had served more than twenty years in the Air Force and had retired from the service as a Lieutenant Colonel. Along with Bill, he had recruited regionally for Air Force Academy and was instrumental in Dan getting an appointment to Air Force. When Bill broke the news that Dan had decided to go to West Point, Myslinski looked at his good friend and smiled.

"What's wrong with that?" he said.

Indeed, Myslinski had once followed his dream to West Point. He played football in the early 1940s, earned consensus All-American as a center in 1943, and graduated from West Point in 1944. He later joined the Air Force and went into sports administration after retiring from the military. If Bill had any doubts whether Myslinski harbored hard feelings over Dan picking Army over Air Force, they were erased when Army hosted Pitt for a football game in 1980.

Dan, in his first year, was a reserve kicker for the Black Knights' football team. The Pitt band played "New York, New York" during halftime and ended its show with "Danny Boy," the famous Irish folk song. Bill, who was at the game with Helen and other family members, couldn't believe it. He later found out that Myslinski had been behind the ode to Dan.

"It stunned us," Bill said. "We were so grateful."

Dan in his Army football uniform and Dan with Woody Hayes after the legendary Ohio State coach spoke at the Black Knights' football banquet.

Another memorable Army football moment involved another of Bill's Pittsburgh connections. Dan served as a captain along with the rest of the seniors when Army played Navy at the historic Rose Bowl in 1983. He took part in the pre-game coin toss in the middle of the field, and Bill's chest swelled with pride more than 3,000 miles away. He was watching from his favorite easy chair in the game room and saw Dan on TV.

Flipping the coin was head referee Gene Steratore.

He and Bill had played football together at Pitt and were friends. Steratore later told Bill that he would have halted the coin toss to say something had he known that Dan was Bill's son. But Dan barely looked at him during the coin toss. Dan wasn't too locked into the game or too caught up in the mystique of the Rose Bowl, and he certainly wasn't being rude. He simply didn't want anyone to think there was anything improper if he said hello to Mr. Steratore.

That was Dan.

F ootball was a fraction of Dan's West Point experience. The demands at a military academy don't allow for specialization, even for the best athletes. Days are filled with classes, drills, and studying. Freshmen quickly learn a harsh arithmetic at West Point: there never seem to be enough hours to get everything done. Adding to the shock is that they are at the bottom at an institution where hierarchy rules.

"It's a big shock to the system," said Dr. Andrew Glen, a 1984 graduate of West Point who was in the same company as Dan. "Going from high school, where you're the king of the mountain, you show up at (West Point) and you're absolutely nobody and they don't want you to be anybody. They don't even care about your name or where you're from. It's kind of humbling to be a nobody even though you know you are a somebody. The result of all of that is you build a team very quickly with the people you are going through this experience with."

Bill and Helen got a glimpse of academy life when they visited Dan his first year for Plebe Parents' Weekend. They were in Dan's dorm room when Bill looked out the window and nearly did a double take. Walking back and forth in full uniform, with a rifle against his shoulder, was a hulking cadet. Dan told Bill that it was Stan March, a defensive tackle and captain on the football team. He was a senior and First Captain of the Corps of Cadets. March was a couple of months away from graduation, yet he was walking off demerits in a marching area. He had received those demerits for being late to class.

"Dad, where else but at West Point would you see this?" Dan said to Bill.

Dan became a Battalion Commander at West Point, like the one shown leading cadets on The Plain. Photo courtesy of United States Military Academy.

The scene reflected the discipline that is the foundation of academy life. It also served as a reminder to Dan that while life would get easier as he adjusted to West Point it would always be a challenge.

"There's almost a science to it," Dan said of academy life. "There are X-number of hours and you learn to maximize them."

He did that at West Point, earning a varsity letter in football as a senior, excelling in his studies, and drawing commendations for his work in military drills. Dan majored in Russian area studies and became so immersed in his major that his fellow cadets nicknamed him, "Little Russian."

"He was a great cadet," said Joseph Bergantz, a 1971 graduate of Army who was a math professor at West Point while Dan was there. "He had very good leadership qualities. You could see he was a strong candidate to go far in the army."

Dan flanked by Helen and Bill his second year at West Point

Dan had limited free time during his years at West Point but that did not stop him from writing regularly to his family. That reflected his desire to stay close to his roots and how he always seemed to think about others.

Barbara Tray, Dan's senior class advisor at Norwin High School, was stunned when she got a letter from Dan after he had gotten a "B" on an English paper. Other students in his class had barely received a passing grade. Dan thanked Tray for those times in sophomore composition class when she made him amend word structure and rewrite papers.

"I can't even tell you how much that touched my heart," Tray said. "He took time out of his day to do that with everything else he had to do at West Point."

The letter only confirmed to Tray how she felt about Dan.

"I never heard anyone, in all the years that I've known him, say anything negative about Danny," she said. "Never once. He was very focused and extremely appreciative of what people did for him."

Dan in his senior class picture at Army. His classmates wrote of him in the yearbook: "The little kicker from Pittsburgh will long be remembered as one who knew more about Russia than the Russians. No one could help but like our first Battalion Commander. He was a good friend who was willing to help those struggling with academics and other problems.

Dan showed that appreciation one Christmas with a gesture that Bill will never forget.

For years, the Priatkos made do with a black-and-white TV. The kids groused about it, especially after their friends started getting color TVs. But Bill and Helen were fine with the old Zenith, even happier if it dissuaded their children from parking themselves in front of the TV.

By the time Dan had settled into West Point, the family TV was approaching relic status. At West Point, cadets are paid for their service though the money can't just be squandered. It is used on uniforms and other things required for academy life. Still, Dan had saved enough money to buy a color TV his sophomore year.

He drove back to North Huntingdon for Christmas break but made a stop before arriving home. Bill was working three jobs at the time and that night he was putting in a shift as a security guard at Russell Standard, a major paving wholesaler in western Pennsylvania. At two o'clock in the morning, Bill heard a knock on the building's front door. Imagine his surprise when he opened the door and saw Dan standing there.

Dan showed Bill the boxed TV that was tied down in the trunk of his car. The look of pride on Dan's face and the gesture itself almost left Bill at a loss for words. His voice caught as he said, "Wait until Mom sees this in the morning!"

Dan gave his parents an even bigger present a couple of years later.

He graduated from West Point on May 26, 1984. Bill and Helen watched with lumpy throats and misted eyes as Dan marched with the other graduates on The Plain as the Army band played, "Auld Lang Syne." They later attached the gold brass pins signifying Dan's rank as Second Lieutenant to his uniform.

Dan at graduation for the Class of 1984 United States Military Academy and
Bill and Helen with Dan in one of their proudest moments as parents

Dan surprised nobody when he took aim at becoming an Army
Ranger. After his acceptance to Ranger school, he again had to navigate
something that separates the elite from the elite.

There were three phases to Ranger school and all of them were
grueling. During the mountain phase, Dan encountered a grizzled
sergeant who told the students, "Nobody changes their socks on me."
Dan's socks got wet while completing a drill in freezing weather, and
he came down with frostbite. He didn't lose any toes but wasn't able
to complete Ranger school. It never occurred to Dan to just move
on. He received a waiver to retake the mountain phase. Dan passed,
and, shortly after graduating from Ranger school, he received his first
assignment.

He never made it to Germany. By the end of March, three weeks
after his accident, doctors concluded that no more could be done for
Dan at Hazleton Hospital.

He was flown to Washington, D.C. and taken by ambulance to Walter Reed Military Medical Center. As in Hazleton, Bill and Helen were with Dan every step of the way. They remained certain that Dan would make a full recovery.

One reason for their optimism was something Dan had done the night before he left for West Point three weeks earlier. Reading his West Point-issued Bible, he had highlighted a passage. It was from Philippians 4:13. It said, "I can do all things through Christ who strengthens me."

Chapter III

WINNERS NEVER QUIT

When Dan arrived at Walter Reed, he was still in a coma. Bill and Helen stayed relentlessly positive, and General Lew Mologne helped them maintain that attitude.

Shortly after Dan got to Walter Reed, Mologne told Bill, "I'll treat him like he's my son."

Bill knew that was not an empty promise from the hospital's head doctor.

The two had met at the same hospital more than three decades earlier when they were trying to get into West Point. Each hailed from western Pennsylvania—Mologne attended Connellsville High School while Bill went to North Braddock Scott High School—and both had arrived for a series of physical and aptitude examinations.

They roomed together and quickly bonded over their roots. Mologne felt comfortable enough to tell Bill that he didn't feel so good about being there. He had just broken up with his girlfriend, and it was still weighing on him.

"Lew, forget her," Bill told him. "Those things happen for the best."

Mologne's childhood sweetheart later became a famous singer and actress. Shirley Jones won an Academy Award in 1960 and in the

1970s played one of the lead roles on the *Partridge Family,* a popular TV sitcom.

Her fame may have eclipsed Mologne, but he did alright too. He graduated from West Point and later Pitt Medical School. Mologne had distinguished himself as a doctor long before he arrived at Walter Reed. Shortly before Dwight D. Eisenhower died in 1969, Mologne was one of twelve doctors on the former U.S. President's team for major surgery. According to Mologne's wife, Rose, Eisenhower ordered that "the only doctor I want to give me my shots or change my IV is the bald-headed West Pointer." Mologne was blessed with many things; a head of hair wasn't one of them. The "bald West Pointer" was among the doctors that Eisenhower, also a West Pointer and a five-star general, called into his hospital room to thank right before he passed.

Mologne rose to the top spot at Walter Reed, turning down a potential nomination to the post of United States Surgeon General along the way. He and Bill had stayed in touch through the years. In late 1984, Bill and Helen visited him and his wife, Rose, in Washington, D.C. Bill told Mologne over dinner that David, Dan's younger brother, needed a medical waiver to get into West Point because of his eyesight. One phone call from Mologne to Army's Keller Hospital was all it took to remove what had been a huge obstacle for David.

General Lewis A. Mologne

Bill and Mologne never imagined they would see each other again just months after that dinner. They certainly didn't want to meet under the circumstances that they did. Mologne's care of Dan confirmed what Bill already knew: he would get things done and be honest with Bill and Helen, especially since he had a son around Dan's age.

A breakthrough occurred at Walter Reed as Dan's family was in his room celebrating Orthodox Easter. His brother and sisters and several other relatives had joined Bill and Helen for the April 14 celebration. They stood around Dan's bed and sang "Christ Is Risen."

At the end of the hymn, Helen said, "Dan's eyes are open!"

Bill, overcome with emotion and adrenaline, shouted, "Look, Dan's eyes are open!"

The room erupted in sobs of happiness. A nurse came running into the room. When she saw Dan, she started crying too.

D r. Philip Dahar, a well-known orthodontist in the Pittsburgh area and former captain of Pitt's football team, always took comfort in the sight of the Veterans Administration (VA) Hospital in Pittsburgh. That, in fact, was one of the reasons why Dahar went to Pitt.

Dahar was a senior in high school when his father, an Air Force veteran, passed away at the VA Hospital in Pittsburgh. Dahar could see the hospital from Pitt Stadium, and he always felt like his father, who was just forty-four when he died, was looking over him. It gave him a sense of peace through his years at Pitt.

He didn't find any solace when he started visiting Dan at the VA Hospital.

Dahar, who had become close to the Priatkos through his work on Dan and David, was devastated by Dan's accident. One day, Dahar told Bill he would give any part of his physical being for Dan to be whole again.

Indeed, Dan still needed a lot of help and perhaps some divine intervention when he arrived at the VA Hospital on May 9. He remained in a coma even though his eyes had stayed open since Easter Sunday. Doctors had no idea whether Dan would have any quality of life because of his traumatic brain injury. One prognosis: He would have the cognitive skills of a three-year-old.

Bill and Helen probably handled Dan's condition better than anyone who visited him in Pittsburgh. It was a struggle for others, especially those dealing with the initial shock of seeing Dan in a vegetative state.

Bob Flaherty had played on the Norwin football scout team with Dan, and memories of his toughness posed an emotional challenge for

Flaherty when he first visited Dan. Flaherty held it together while he was in Dan's room. As soon as he returned to his car, he broke down crying.

Greg Petrick grappled with similar emotions. He and Dan had pushed each other since junior high, becoming best friends and receiving appointments to the Air Force Academy. They had taken different but similar paths. Each was supposed to serve his country with distinction. Petrick was on his way to doing that. Dan was lying in a hospital bed, tubes crisscrossing his supine body.

"That was not the guy I knew, and for me that was awfully hard to accept," Petrick said. "There were probably opportunities to go see Dan where I didn't. That was more my problem than Dan's problem."

Former teammates, such as Hugh Campbell, Dan's cousin; Rick Gaudino; and Mark Critz visited Dan regularly. They would stand near his bed and spin old football and school stories, hoping the guy they had once tagged with the nickname "Onions" because of the lines from his closely cropped haircuts could hear them.

Family members and friends weren't the only ones to watch over Dan. Mary Jane McKnight, a veteran of World War II, was in the VA Hospital the same time as Dan. She became something of a mother hen; eyes and ears for when Bill and Helen couldn't be there. She watched over Dan the five months he spent in the VA Hospital, making sure he got the proper care and reporting to Bill and Helen when she thought he wasn't getting enough medical attention.

Her attentiveness and the love she developed for Dan reflected the support for the Priatkos that seemingly came from every source. It started at home with Dan's three siblings.

"Whatever we were doing to support Dan or be with Dan, they were right behind us," Bill said. "They never complained or felt any sense of being neglected because we always did a lot of things together."

Bill and Helen needed that togetherness more than ever after the family received more devastating news.

Helen had experienced a health scare a couple of years before Dan's accident when a cluster of cysts were discovered on her breasts. The cysts were initially benign but eventually turned cancerous.

A couple of months after breast-removal surgery, Helen was diagnosed with terminal bladder cancer. A urological specialist told her the cancer was so advanced that she should start preparing for the end. Such news, coming with Dan still in a coma, would have overwhelmed many people. It didn't even cause Helen's knees to wobble.

"I don't believe him," she told Bill after they left the doctor's office. "I won't accept that."

They sought a second opinion from Dr. James McCague. The renowned urological specialist examined Helen and, with a smile, told her to put the funeral arrangements on hold. Helen started chemotherapy and radiation treatment and stayed at Presbyterian Hospital while Dan was still in the VA Hospital.

Her cancer loomed over the family as Dan was transferred from the VA Hospital, where he had stayed for nearly five months, to Harmarville Rehabilitation Center on October 4. Dan was awake when he arrived at Harmarville but still in a semi-coma since he wasn't always lucid. He could talk a little but didn't make much sense.

Yet that didn't stop Dan from providing hope to his parents.

Early at Harmarville, Dan wrote on a piece of paper: "Winners never quit and quitters never win." Bill was stunned when he found it in Dan's room.

Dan writing it then seemed to be his message to Bill and Helen that everything would be all right, that sheer grit and determination would allow him to overcome the car accident that should have killed him.

A couple of weeks later Dan surprised his parents again when he wrote a poem that he titled "Storm to Rainbow":

Have you ever observed how after a terrible storm,
There is a beautiful rainbow grandly arching over the sky?
The incidents in our life are a remarkable parallel
Like the storm we suffer a seemingly insurmountable blow
But just when we reach our emotional low a bright rainbow appears
To one who is willing to listen the message is obviously clear
The same God who turns a storm into a magnificent rainbow
Can transform a dark today into a bright tomorrow

That Dan could write something so poignant when his verbal skills
were still so rudimentary defied logic. Bill nearly broke down crying when
he read it. A couple of weeks later, he and Helen received the second
breakthrough they had coveted since Easter Sunday.

They were in Dan's room talking about her latest chemotherapy treatment. Doctors still did not think Dan could hear, and Bill and Helen were
sure he couldn't hear them as they talked quietly about Helen's cancer.

They could have been forgiven if they thought they were dreaming
when Dan lifted his head from his pillow.

"Mom?" he said.

Bill and Helen, sitting next to Dan's bed, looked at him speechless.

"You and I are going to whip this thing together," he said.

David Alexander Priatko was born four years after Dan. Just as Dan's
middle name of Andrew was in honor of Bill's father, David's
middle name was in honor of Helen's father.

David, like many younger brothers, became Dan's shadow from the
time he could walk. He tagged after him everywhere and took after him
in just about everything. When Dan became too busy with sports in
junior high to continue his paper routes, David took them over. When

Dan's friends gave him the nickname "Onions," David naturally became "Onions Junior."

Like Dan, David served as class president and evolved into a young man with the manners of a Boy Scout and the tenacity of a pit bull.

David even followed Dan in using his right leg to produce a dramatic win for Norwin's football team. David kicked for Norwin in addition to playing running back. As a senior, a rivalry game at neighboring Penn-Trafford High School produced a standing room only crowd and a white-knuckle finish. Norwin needed a field goal to win and moved the ball to Penn-Trafford's twenty-yard line.

The drive stalled, and David trotted onto the field to attempt a 37-yard field goal. Bill was watching the game with Norwin principal Ron Peduzzi and Penn-Trafford principal Rey Peduzzi. Bill flashed back to Dan attempting an extra point that Norwin needed to beat Latrobe. Watching with frayed nerves, Bill hoped David could do the same, albeit from a much farther distance.

"Why do fathers have to go through this?" Bill said to the Peduzzi brothers.

Penn-Trafford added to Bill's angst by calling a timeout to give David time to think about the stakes. It didn't work. David drilled the kick that delivered the win and calmed Bill's beating heart.

Given how much David idolized Dan, it came as no surprise that he was determined to follow him to West Point. That is why what should have been one of the best days of his young life turned into one of the worst.

On the day of his high school graduation, David received a letter from West Point denying his application. He had received a Congressional nomination, but his eyesight hadn't met the baseline requirement. David got the bad new hours before he was scheduled to speak at graduation. He carried out his duties as class president, crestfallen as he was, but was left to ponder an uncertain future.

David had been offered a full Marine Corps ROTC scholarship. He could have had many other options as well with grades and extra-curricular activities that distinguished him from most students. But David only had eyes for West Point. He decided to bet on himself in part because of Dan.

All his life David had seen Dan succeed. That could have cast a shadow that caused David to wilt under the pressure. Instead, Dan's example shaped David. It convinced him that anything was possible through determination and faith.

He passed on the options available to him after graduation and enrolled at Westmoreland County Community College. The plan was to take classes for a year and double back on West Point. And Plan B? There was none.

His family fully backed David's pursuit of West Point. Dan wrote a letter to his brother when David's future was uncertain. It was during the summer when Dan was at artillery training school in Oklahoma. Dan told David that if he really wanted to go to West Point, he could accomplish it through hard work.

"That was the encouragement I really needed at that time," David said.

He stayed singularly focused on West Point, but such resolve couldn't change one fundamental truth: getting into West Point was still beyond what he could control. David couldn't improve his vision— this was years before Lasik surgery became a viable option —and he needed another Congressional nomination. There was never a shortage of qualified candidates for military academies so it was fair to wonder if David could get a second nomination when he hadn't gotten into West Point the first time.

He got some help from Pittsburgh Steelers president Dan Rooney, who knew Bill from his time with the Steelers. Rooney successfully lobbied Pennsylvania U.S. Representative John F. Murtha for a nomination on David's behalf.

General Lew Mologne took care of the rest by ordering that David receive a medical waiver, something Bill didn't tell David about until years later.

David got accepted to West Point on Jan. 26, 1985. A week later, Mologne wrote him a note on paper with two stars on top of it, signifying his rank as Major General: "Dear David, Welcome to the fraternity. You're now a member of the Long Gray Line."

David wrote a letter back that included this passage: "Words cannot adequately express my feelings on receiving an appointment to West Point and the appreciation I feel toward those who helped me to achieve this goal. Thank you so much. I look forward to meeting the challenge of The Long Gray Line and proudly serving my country as an Army officer."

David left for initial training in July 1985, four months after Dan's catastrophic accident. He arrived at West Point with purpose beyond vindicating those who had helped him with his second chance.

He might have to finish what Dan had started.

By Thanksgiving, Dan still at Harmarville Rehabilitation Center, was deemed well enough to return home for the holiday. David also came home for the first time since leaving for West Point.

He arrived wearing his wool gray uniform. With tears in his eyes, he approached his older brother in the family game room. The two hugged as their parents and sisters watched.

Dan's brain was still so damaged that he couldn't physically cry, but his family knew he grasped the magnitude of the moment. Dan shook with emotion from the moment he saw David dressed in his Army uniform through their emotional hug. It was his way of crying without the tears.

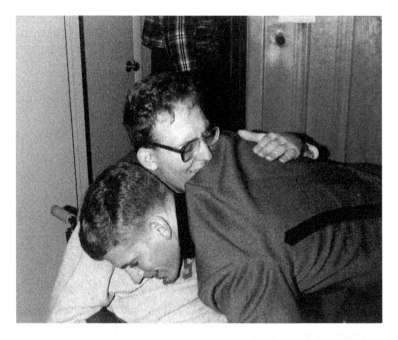

Dan and David share a hug that was emotional for the entire Priatko family.

Debbie, the oldest of the Priatko children, may have cherished that moment as much as her brothers. She had been in the accident with Dan and had suffered less severe injuries. What proved to be more lasting was the emotional trauma from the accident. Debbie had to pull over on the ride back to North Huntingdon one time after visiting Dan at Walter Reed Military Medical Center. A freak snowstorm hit, and it triggered memories of the accident with Dan. It took a year for Debbie to drive when there was snow or rain without feeling panicked.

That didn't stop her from exhibiting the fortitude her family needed.

Debbie worked at Children's Hospital of Pittsburgh, and after work she went to the VA Hospital to be with Dan or Presbyterian Hospital to be with Helen.

She and Bill made sure one of them was always with Dan and Helen. They often left Pittsburgh at eleven o'clock at night, zipping through a McDonald's drive-thru on the way home since neither had had time for dinner earlier. The days were exhausting, and Debbie essentially put her life on hold.

Seeing Dan and David's reunion made it all worth it.

D avid's visit wasn't the only reminder of how much West Point meant to Dan and his family.

A week after Thanksgiving, Army's men's basketball team visited Robert Morris University. Bill had a deep appreciation for both. Since Dan's accident, the support from West Point had been unwavering. Robert Morris had also helped immensely. Bill had been working at the Pittsburgh-area school for less than three years when Dan had his accident. Bill did not have significant sick or leave time accumulated. Yet, the school paid him for eight months while he took off work. This allowed him to focus on Dan as he went from Hazleton Hospital to Walter Reed Military Medical Center to Harmarville Rehabilitation Center and to help care for Helen after she was diagnosed with bladder cancer.

"They paid me every penny like I was working," Bill said.

Bill had hoped to take Dan to the Army-Robert Morris game, but it was too cold for him to leave Harmarville that night.

The teams played a close game with a wild finish. Gene Steratore, who had handled the pre-game coin toss at the Rose Bowl when Dan served as a captain for the Army-Navy game, was one of the referees. He probably wanted to get out of the building as quickly as possible after Army beat Robert Morris, 51-50.

Bill stayed after the game. He saw something that almost took his breath away. All fifteen Army players came out of the visiting locker room and formed a line. They walked in lockstep before stopping in front of Bill.

"Mr. Priatko, I'm Mark Michaelsen," the player at the head of the line said. "I'm the team captain. You tell Dan he's part of our chain. We're all together."

He handed Bill a black and gold mesh basketball jersey. The chain on the front of the jersey circled around the words "Only Together."

Bill also left that night with an Army media guide. It was signed to Dan by every team member. Kevin Houston, who would lead all Division I players in scoring that season, wrote, "Glad to see you're improving. Keep up the great spirit you have shown. The Army team and their thoughts are always with you."

As Bill drove home, he couldn't stop thinking about the gesture, the chain on the jersey and "Only Together." Dan's alma mater had proven once again that those words truly mean something to West Pointers.

Dorothy Tragesser knew about Dan, but she had never met him before working with him as his speech therapist in the summer of 1986.

Dan had finally returned home, fourteen months after his accident. That triumph was somewhat tempered by Bill and Helen coming to terms with the reality that Dan would not make it all the way back. They had clung to the belief that Dan would one day return to the Army, to the life he had in front of him before the terrible accident.

Unfortunately, a series of MRIs showed that his brain had been irreparably damaged in some areas. Dr. Lew Mologne told Bill and Helen that they had to adjust their expectations now a year after the accident. Basics such as walking, talking, and sleeping would always be a struggle for Dan.

The one thing the accident did not change was the can-do strand in Dan's DNA. Dan approached his rehabilitation the same way he had

West Point and Army Ranger School. Obstacles were to be overcome, not shied away from. That code had always guided Dan. It was the only way he knew how to live.

Tragesser assumed since Dan had been in some form of a coma for fourteen months that he had a steep and possibly insurmountable climb ahead. Her training and experience told her how layered the issues were that Dan was facing just to talk again.

"The thing about a traumatic brain injury is, when you look at communication, it's not just the way somebody talks. You can have such problems with your intellect that you can't retrieve your words," Tragesser said. "You're drawing a blank all the time or you can't arrange words into a coherent sentence. You have no filters. You just say whatever comes to your mind. Maybe you can't read facial expressions. There's just so many things."

Her first day working with Dan raised her expectations dramatically.

"I go there and find a person whose intellect is not only intact but what a fabulous sense of humor," she said. "I was just absolutely blown away at what a high level he was functioning."

Dan turned out to be a "dream patient" for Tragesser. She became a critical part of his support team, a cast that also featured his immediate family and the community.

Norwin allowed the Priatkos to use the high school after classes were finished for the day. The long hallways were perfect for Dan to work on his walking. One time his younger sister Kathy was with Dan, holding his hand as he took one deliberate step after another. John Polivka, Dan's favorite Norwin teacher, had stayed late that day and saw the two as he was leaving.

Polivka was unaware of Dan's accident, but recognized Kathy. Figuring it had to be Dan with her, he was so stunned that he could not approach them. When Polivka found out what had happened, it shook him.

"It was difficult to even learn that something like this had happened to him," Polivka said. "I just felt so bad because the kid had so much promise. It hurt me."

But Dan never wallowed in self-pity, never asked why him. He always kept his focus forward. Sometimes he got a little too far ahead of himself.

Norwin had also allowed the Priatkos to use the football field for Dan to walk. When his physical therapist found out that Bill was letting him walk goal-line to goal-line without a cane or any other assistance, he was apoplectic. He told Bill that Dan wasn't physically up to doing that yet. It was one of the few concessions Dan reluctantly made to the accident. Indeed, Shirley Yohman, who lives next-door to the Priatkos, would see Dan working on his walking on the driveway. His physical therapist would not have been any happier hearing about that. The driveway is concrete and sloped. But Dan would be out there with a quad cane, grinding away and never knowing that his next-door neighbor sometimes watched with bated breath because she was worried that he would fall and break something.

"I often wondered how he did it," Yohman said, "but he seemed to have a lot of courage."

One goal that Dan set soon after he returned home involved a place that he considered a second home.

Dan had grown up in St. Nicholas Orthodox Church in Donora, serving as an altar boy and signing in the choir. His accident showed just how tight the bond was among the parishioners. Julia Drahushak and the Petro family were among those who led prayer efforts and lit vigil candles for Dan (Drahushak later became a member of the sprawling Petro family when her daughter married into it).

Dr. Dmitri Petro's parents were among the founders of the church, and Petro is an institution at the church and within the community. A well-respected medical doctor, he has been Ringgold High School football team's doctor for more than fifty years. That means he was at the school when it was Donora High School and, of course, later when a quarterback by the name of Joe Montana starred at Ringgold. Petro has also been the choir director at St. Nicholas for more than fifty years and always refused any attempts by the church to pay him for those services.

Petro watched the Priatko children come of age and was devastated when he learned of Dan's accident.

"He was the kind of guy that you want your daughter to bring home on a date," Petro said. "He's just a wonderful example for everyone in the church."

The first time Dan returned to church he walked slowly and wobbly yet made it and took Communion. The congregation, which had prayed for Dan every week since the accident, dissolved into tears.

"That was very touching seeing him in church," Petro said, "and we were amazed at how far he had come."

The Priatko family with Father Igor Soroka in front of St. Nicholas Orthodox Church in Donora, Pennsylvania. From left to right: Debbie, Kathy, Dan, Helen, Bill, and David.

Father Igor Soroka had promised Dan that as soon as he was able, he would have him read the Epistle during a service. It would be a real test since Dan would have to walk, stand, and then read the scripture lesson.

Dan labored through it, but Bill was right next to him the whole time, patiently encouraging Dan and helping him through it.

"It was very emotional," Bill said.

To Bill, it was another marker for how far Dan had come from those days when doctors never thought he would live or that he would have no quality of life if he did pull through.

To Dan, it was simply another figurative step. He had more places to go, more people to show as he continued his fight back from catastrophe.

D an never remembered the six weeks he spent at Walter Reed National Military Medical Center. He got an idea of how bad his condition had been while there during a visit with General Lew Mologne.

Three years after Dan's stay at Walter Reed, where Mologne had been the head doctor, and Mologne was in Pittsburgh awaiting a liver transplant. Mologne was sitting in the corner of his Presbyterian Hospital room when Bill and Dan walked in. His face lit up; his arms shot to the ceiling.

"Dan! Dan!" he said with clenched fists and tears in his eyes. "God, it's good to see you!"

Dan, now walking with the aid of a quad cane, and Bill spent several hours with Mologne. Bill returned the following day and asked Mologne to level with him. Bill sensed his friend's health problems went beyond needing a new liver due to the hepatitis Mologne had contracted from treating a soldier who had been wounded in Vietnam. "I've got this dang blasted cancer," he told Bill.

Mologne, who was only fifty-six, had the transplant but the cancer was too far advanced. Shortly after Dan and Bill visited him, Mologne was transferred back to Walter Reed where doctors tried to make him as comfortable as possible.

Rose Mologne called Bill in July 1988 to tell him that her husband was really slipping. Bill told her Dan wanted to write Mologne a letter. "Tell Dan to do it in a hurry," she said.

This is what he wrote:

Dear General Mologne,

"Duty-Honor-Country. Those three hallowed words reverently dictate what you ought to be, what you can be, what you will be." Sir, in your case, "...what you will be" can be replaced by what you are. You are the exemplification of the officer MacArthur envisioned when he spoke these words.

Sir, I will be eternally grateful for all you have done for me. "Give and it shall be given to you," God promised. Based on those words, General Mologne, you are a clear victor and your prize awaits you.

With respect and the love of Christ,
Dan Priatko

Mologne died on Aug. 1. He was buried next to Walter Reed in Arlington National Cemetery. Bill and Helen drove to Washington, D.C. for his funeral.

Rose told them that Lew read Dan's letter right before he passed.

"That meant an awful lot to my husband," Rose Mologne recalled nearly thirty years after his death. "There was such a bond there with Dan, the West Pointer, and my husband, the physician, the West Pointer."

That West Point bond could be seen through another well-known doctor who took an interest in Dan.

Dr. John Hutton, Jr. stopped in Dan's room one day while he was at Walter Reed. Hutton was President Ronald Reagan's personal physician, and he had a connection to Dan through his son.

John Hutton III and Dan had been classmates at West Point. Hutton had also been a manager for the football team and had shagged Dan's kicks in practice. Hutton's father wanted to support Dan and his family. Hutton stopped at Walter Reed several times to check on Dan, and he stayed in touch with the Priatkos.

He also told President Reagan about Dan, and Dan's story left an impression on the leader of the free world.

In January 1989, with just a few weeks remaining in his presidency, Reagan asked Hutton how "Dan Priatko" was doing. Hutton told Reagan that he would find out right away. Hutton called Bill, telling him that Reagan had asked about Dan. He also told Bill that he was retiring and moving to Seattle, which was another reason why he had phoned him.

"I just wanted to call you to make you aware that Dan will never be forgotten," Hutton said.

A couple of days later, a package arrived at the Priatko house from the White House. It contained an autographed picture of Ronald and Nancy Reagan.

To Dan
with every good wish,

Nancy + *Ronald Reagan*

Ronald and Nancy Reagan sent this to Dan shortly before President Reagan
left office in 1989.

Six months later something happened that Bill would have considered as unlikely as the President of the United States asking about his
son and then sending a treasured keepsake.

Bill was working at Robert Morris where college basketball coaches
had converged for the annual Five-Star Basketball Camp.

Duke University's Mike Krzyzewski was on the cusp of great-
ness when Bill approached him with an old Army men's basketball
media guide. Krzyzewski, who was leaving for Pittsburgh International
Airport, stopped to look at a full-length picture in the back of the guide.

It showed a twentysomething head coach by the name of Bobby Knight with his captain, a heady point guard with a Polish name that was as hard to spell as it was to pronounce. Krzyzewski smiled when he saw the picture. He and Bill started talking. Krzyzewski said it sounded like Bill knew something about West Point. Bill told him that he had two sons who, like Krzyzewski, had graduated from there. He also told him about Dan's accident.

"Come on," Krzyzewski said after hearing the story. "I want to meet him."

Bill was flabbergasted when he realized Krzyzewski was serious. The Priatkos lived on the other side of Pittsburgh and, with rush hour traffic, Krzyzewski would never make it to the airport in time. Krzyzewski said he would take a later flight. When Bill asked why he was so insistent on meeting Dan, Krzyzewski said, "He's a West Pointer, isn't he?"

Bill thanked him profusely but said he couldn't let him do it. Krzyzewski finally relented and signed the media guide picture: "To Dan and Dave, From one West Pointer to two others. Best of luck, Mike Krzyzewski."

It could have ended right there. Instead, it marked the start of a beautiful friendship.

Chapter IV

Roots of Strength

Love almost killed Bill Priatko in 1950. He was in his first year at Pitt, serving as a captain for the unbeaten freshmen football team and getting ready for a big game against visiting Penn State. A storm walloped Pittsburgh, dumping thirty-six inches of snow on the city.

The freshman game was cancelled. The varsity game, also scheduled for the day after Thanksgiving, was moved to the following week and from Pitt Stadium to Forbes Field. The snow shut down the street cars that served as Pittsburgh's main source of public transportation. Cars that had slid into snowbanks or been rendered undrivable dotted the roads in and around the city.

Union Railroad hired scores of temporary workers to help clear the tracks. With his freshman game cancelled, Bill decided to make a couple of bucks shoveling snow. A week earlier, Bill had suffered a minor injury during a win against West Virginia. He got cleated on his left calf, leaving a small cut. Bill stayed in the game, but the cut became infected unbeknownst to Bill. Shoveling snow for hours that week made it worse.

What almost proved fatal was when Bill couldn't wait any longer to see his girlfriend. Helen Dutka lived two miles away in Braddock, and the streets were still a mess. Bill didn't care.

He was young. He was in love. But he was also seventeen years old and, by definition, short-sighted. He trudged to Helen's house, not knowing that every step there and back put him closer to death.

A couple of days later, Bill woke up and knew something was terribly wrong. His calf throbbed with pain and the room spun even as he laid in bed. He didn't move, even after his mother said, "Billy, get down here! Sweep the cellar!"

When he did not answer, his mother walked into his room. All it took was one look at the youngest of her three sons for her to rush to the phone.

As soon as the family doctor arrived, he told Bill's mother to call an ambulance. Bill drifted in and out of consciousness as he was rushed to Mercy Hospital in Pittsburgh. He got there just in time for doctors to stem the infection that had seeped into his blood.

A couple of days later, a doctor told him, "Son, if they would have brought you here one hour later, you were gone."

Bill spent ten days in the hospital as antibiotics coursed through his body. What saved him was that he was young and so strong.

At least he hadn't flirted with death over some fleeting teenage infatuation.

Bill and Helen were seemingly meant to be from the time they were barely old enough to walk. Each attended Holy Resurrection Orthodox Church in Braddock, and Bill first noticed Helen when they were toddlers. His father always gave him strict instructions in Slavonic to "ticho byt." That meant sit there and be quiet. He never had to tell Bill twice.

"But out of the corner of my eye I could see this little blond-haired girl and that started it," Bill recalled. "That was the spark."

That spark nearly fizzled because Bill simply did not have time for girls growing up. Sports consumed him. He played football, basketball, and baseball. He also had family responsibilities thrust on him at a young age because of his father's death.

Andrew Pratko had emigrated to the United States as a seventeen-year-old from the Ukraine. By the time he got through processing at Ellis Island an "i" had been inserted into his surname. That explained why Bill grew up near a first cousin with the last name Pratko.

Andrew Priatko was a coal miner and he migrated to Clymer, Pennsylvania, just outside of Indiana. There, he met Catherine Pohlut, who was eighteen years his junior. They married when he was thirty-four and she was sixteen. A series of strikes compelled them to move to North Braddock where Andrew found work in a steel mill.

Like many immigrants of his generation in western Pennsylvania, Andrew Priatko was shaped by long, grueling hours in the mills. His toughness may have killed him.

Andrew Priatko shoveled snow one December day in 1937 wearing a white undershirt and no coat. He caught pneumonia and got so sick that he finally went to Braddock Hospital. He died there at age forty-seven, leaving a twenty-nine-year-old wife to raise five kids, including six-year-old Bill. He was buried two days before Christmas.

The death of the family patriarch meant everyone had to help keep food on the table. All three Priatko brothers had paper routes and sold hard-boiled eggs. Bill's older brother, John, swept borough streets to make money for the family. In addition to those jobs, the three brothers shared a chore that their mother insisted be done daily when the weather permitted: water the flowers around Andrew Priatko's grave. It was a two-mile walk roundtrip to the cemetery but there was never any arguing with her about it.

"No matter what we were doing, we had to cut it short and get that big (watering) can," Bill said.

Sports and family responsibilities left little time for much else. That is why Bill turned down Helen several times when she asked him to accompany her to a dance or on a hayride. It might have cost him a future with her if his sister Terry had not intervened.

One day Terry said to Bill, "Helen told me she's going to ask you one more time, and if you don't go out with her that's it."

Bill finally got the message. Once he and Helen started dating, he fell hard. He knew there was no other girl for him and wanted to marry Helen while he attended Pitt. His mother told him he was too young, but it was clear that the two would one day be husband and wife.

They were married May 18, 1957 at the church where Bill had once furtively snuck glances at Helen. It was drizzling when they got to the church. During the ceremony, the priest offered words that turned out to be prophetic.

Bill and Helen on their wedding day on May 18, 1957

"You're going to have dark clouds and rain and then you're going to have sunshine," he said. "And you're going to learn to handle it."

When they emerged from the church as Mr. and Mrs. William Priatko, the sun was out. There wasn't a cloud in the sky.

Sid Gillman is rightfully considered one of the fathers of modern football. While coach of the San Diego Chargers in the 1960s, he established himself as the Frank Lloyd Wright of the downfield passing game. His innovations helped revolutionized the game, slowly transforming it from plodding, run-dominant offenses to sleek passing outfits that eventually dominated the sport.

Long before he rose to prominence with his offensive philosophy, Gillman was the head coach at the University of Cincinnati, and he wanted Bill Priatko.

Bill starred at North Braddock Scott High School as a guard and defensive end/linebacker. He had size, toughness, and an uncanny nose for the ball. One game he recorded almost thirty tackles. He seemed like a man among boys even if he was younger than most of his classmates. Bill had started lifting weights at the age of twelve and became so strong that he could do 300 consecutive push-ups. A handful of Division I schools heavily courted him, including Cincinnati, Virginia Tech, Maryland, and Pitt.

Paul Dietzel, a Cincinnati assistant coach, visited Bill every Saturday morning during the recruiting process. He recruited Catherine Priatko nearly as hard as he did Bill, correctly reading that Mom would be a major factor in his decision.

Pitt assistant coach Steve Petro played Bill's recruitment a tad bit better. He always seemed to show up at the Priatko house shortly after Dietzel left so he could have the final word. He never failed to ask "Mrs. Priatko" if Bill was "domo," which is Slovak for home.

"My mom took to Steve Petro because he spoke to her in her language," Bill said.

Pitt eventually overtook Cincinnati as Bill's top choice, and he accepted a full athletic scholarship from the Panthers. Bill was just sixteen years old when he graduated from high school in 1949. His football coach convinced him to put off college for a year so his age would not be a disadvantage when he got to Pitt.

Bill entered Pitt in 1950, just a couple of months after war broke out in Korea. At Pitt, like schools across the country, freshmen football players were subject to the draft. They also had the option of joining the Reserve Officer Training Corps (ROTC) followed by a three-year military commitment that precluded them from getting drafted. Bill joined the Air Force ROTC and spent all four years at Pitt in that program. He distinguished himself on the freshmen team (freshmen were still decades away from being eligible to play for the varsity) and became a three-year starter at defensive tackle and guard.

He played well enough that Bolling Air Force Base in Washington, D.C. wanted him to play football and serve in its Honor Guard after Bill spent a year in Air Force training schools.

The military teams were filled with men who had played in the NFL, due to a commonly used deferment, before serving their three-year military commitment. Bill played one season for Bolling and all but one of the eleven starters (they played both ways) had NFL experience. Bill was the lone exception.

One of his teammates was former Notre Dame halfback Johnny Lattner, the seventh overall pick of the NFL draft in 1954. Lattner played one season for the Pittsburgh Steelers, earning Pro Bowl honors as a kick returner before reporting to Bolling for his military commitment. Unfortunately, he sustained a career-ending knee injury while playing for Bolling.

Bill won a National Service Championship at Bolling and made the All-Service team as a center/linebacker. Those honors came at the apex of military football, gaining Bill plenty of exposure.

"It was good football," Bill said. "All of our games were on TV. We got more coverage playing in Washington than the Redskins."

If playing for Bolling was invaluable—it allowed Bill to continue developing with an eye toward the NFL—the military experience was priceless. Bill served in President Dwight D. Eisenhower's Honor Guard and was also the officer in charge of Air Force funerals at Arlington Cemetery.

It wouldn't surprise anyone who knows Bill that he often made small talk with Eisenhower when they were together. After he won re-election in 1956, Eisenhower requested that Bill serve as the lead officer of the forty-four men who guarded the presidential ball. Helen watched the inauguration festivities on TV and saw Bill talking to Lawrence Welk.

"Greatest experience of my life to be in President Eisenhower's Honor Guard and to conduct Air Force funerals at Arlington Cemetery," Bill said.

Bill (top) on duty at Washington National Airport. Bill (bottom right) is congratulated after getting selected to lead the Air Force Honor Guard at President Dwight D. Eisenhower's inaugural ball.

An early release from his Air Force commitment allowed Bill to pursue an NFL career. He signed with the Green Bay Packers for $7,500. The $500 signing bonus that Bill received paid for his and Helen's wedding. A couple of months later, Bill reported to training camp in Wisconsin.

He made the team coming out of camp but got caught in a numbers crunch.

Carlton Massey, an All-Pro linebacker for the Packers, got an early release from the Army National Guard and reported to Green Bay in September. His return relegated Bill to the taxi squad, the forerunner to the NFL practice squads that allow teams to keep players who are not on the active roster.

The Steelers signed Bill from the Packers' taxi squad. He was thrilled to be returning home. Since the season had already started, Bill signed a

$5,500 prorated contract – or $458 a game. Bill played for the Steelers that season and a couple of years later Sid Gillman came back into his life.

Gillman wanted to sign Bill in 1960, and Bill was convinced that assistant coach Al Davis had offered him a $10,000 no-cut contract. Davis claimed while Bill was visiting the Chargers that he had never offered a no-cut provision. Without that protection, Bill figured he would just be another body for training camp. What infuriated him was his belief that Davis had gone back on his word.

He left Los Angeles abruptly. Another of Gillman's assistant coaches, Chuck Noll, tried to repair the damage and sign Bill. He was the right person for Gillman to send to Pittsburgh. Bill and Noll had gotten close during 1959 training camp with the Browns. Both were linebackers (Noll also played some guard) and ate dinner together every night. They got to know each other as more than just players. As with Dick LeBeau, his roommate at camp. Bill's time with the Browns laid the foundation for a lifelong friendship.

"We talked about everything but football," Bill said of Noll. "We really had deep discussions."

Noll retired after the 1959 season and joined Gillman's staff. He and Bill met at a Hilton Hotel in Pittsburgh after the Davis flap, but Noll could not get him to reconsider signing. With Bill, it was a matter of principle; he refused to have anything to do with Davis.

His football career ended when he tore a quadriceps muscle while playing for the Browns in 1960. Despite having his career cut short at twenty-nine, Bill took many positives from his NFL career. In addition to LeBeau and Noll, he became good friends with Green Bay Packers quarterback Bart Starr. The two regularly wrote to each other prior to Starr's death in 2019.

He also stayed in touch with Cleveland coach Paul Brown. It had pained Brown to release Bill after he tore his quadriceps. He said as much on his weekly radio show. Brown also said that he thought Bill could have played ten seasons for Cleveland if not for the injury.

Brown, one of the NFL's legendary coaches, would later come through for Bill when he needed it most.

Bill had his share of professional hard luck after his football career ended.

He had worked as a regional salesman for Wrigley while playing in the NFL, and it was a good job. He had a company car, an expense account, and made considerably more money than what most NFL players earned at the time. The company also allowed Bill to take leaves of absence for football.

Bill was a natural at sales, but something was missing from the job. He yearned to teach and coach, to make an impact on young people. That is why he left Wrigley after twelve years with the chewing gum company, returning to Pitt to get his teaching certificate and a master's degree in education.

Armed with those, he landed a job at nearby California State College (now California University) in 1970 as an assistant dean of men and assistant football coach.

Bill loved the job, and the students he mentored and the players he coached loved him. It was a perfect fit until Cal State hired a new president during Bill's first year. The president mandated that all dean of men had to live in the city of California. The reasoning behind the new policy was to have them nearby in case there was trouble in the dormitories.

Bill did not want to move his family from the house and neighborhood they had grown to love. The president would make no exceptions, even after three dormitory resident assistants lobbied for Bill to stay.

"We admired him and respected him and thought he was the greatest guy for that job," said Mike Siyufy, one of the resident assistants who met with the president on Bill's behalf.

When it became clear that Bill had to leave after one year at Cal State, students took up a collection. They raised over $100 dollars and bought him a blazer. They gave it to him during a farewell reception.

"He was deeply touched and pretty much at a loss for words," recalled Henry Heer, another of the resident assistants who fought for Bill to stay.

Bill found a job closer to home, teaching history and coaching the football team at Swissvale High School.

He loved the job but couldn't resist the pull of the military when the Air Force approached him about returning to active duty. He spent six months as a New Jersey-based recruiter for the Mid-Atlantic region. He worked the last year of the job at home after Pittsburgh became his base of operations.

Bill retired from the Air Force with honors and a full pension after the assignment ended. He got a job teaching at General Braddock High School. After a year, General Braddock merged with a handful of schools to form Woodland Hills High School, which would famously turn into a pipeline for the NFL. The consolidation eliminated scores of teaching jobs. As one of the least-tenured teachers at General Braddock, Bill found himself out of a job.

He quickly found work as a recruiting director at the sprawling Volkswagen manufacturing plant in New Stanton. It was a good job at one of the biggest manufacturing centers and a major employer in western Pennsylvania. The plant manager met with Bill one day to tell him that the company wanted to groom him for a labor relations position.

The offer came with a couple of catches. One, it wasn't an offer as much as a take-it-or-leave-the-company proposition. Bill would have gladly accepted the promotion, but his boss wanted him to work from 4:00 p.m. to 3:00 a.m. the first couple of years. That was the lightest of the three shifts at the plant and the best time to train Bill and break him in on the new job.

Bill flatly refused the promotion. His stunned boss told him that he could make good money, but Bill did not want to miss his kids' sporting events.

Bill left Volkswagen without a safety net and spent the next couple of years struggling to make ends meet. He worked full-time as a substitute teacher at Norwin High School, but that only paid $11,000 a year. He supplemented that income by loading trucks every Friday and Sunday from midnight to 8 a.m. at a local warehouse. He worked Saturdays as a security guard at a nearby McDonald's and Russell Standard.

Bill did not teach in the summer but still spent long shifts working as a security guard and bricklayer and loading trucks. His youngest daughter, Kathy, got up one summer morning in 1981 at 4 o'clock for Lady Diana Spencer's marriage to Prince Charles. She was watching the royal wedding when Bill got home from one of his jobs. That snapshot went beyond a tired father returning home after a long night of work.

Two years earlier, Lebanon Valley College had offered Bill a job as an assistant football coach and administrator. It seemed to be the answer to his and Helen's prayers. He loved coaching and loved being around kids. The job would have alleviated the family's financial strain and allowed Bill to get more than a couple of hours of sleep a night. But it would have required Bill to move his family across the state near Harrisburg.

Dan was going into his senior year at Norwin. He was going to be a captain on the football team and class president. Bill didn't want Dan to miss that. *He* didn't want to miss that, which is why he turned down the job offer.

Bill continued sending out resumes by the hundreds but wondered if the fact that he was fifty-one years old worked against him getting the kind of job he coveted. In 1982, Bill applied for an assistant athletic director position at Robert Morris University. Paul Brown found out about it from a mutual friend.

Brown called Robert Morris President Charles L. Sewall with whom he enjoyed more than just name recognition. Sewall had grown up idolizing Brown, and Brown gave Bill, his former player, a glowing recommendation. Shortly after that phone conversation, Sewall called Robert Morris' human resources department and said to hire Bill.

"He pulled me out of economic chaos in my life," Bill said of Brown. "I was so grateful for him being so good to me."

The job provided the financial stability that Bill and the Priatkos had not had since he left Volkswagen. He was also back working with kids and in athletics. Dan was in his junior year at West Point and thriving. His other kids were happy and doing well. Finally, it seemed everything had come together for the Priatkos.

Helen never learned how to drive. That was one of the few things she didn't do.

If the dishwasher broke down, the kids were certain to see Helen poking around inside of it with a screwdriver. She could fix just about anything.

She was just as handy with money. To the penny, Helen knew how much money the family had. She also got the most out of interest rates and coupons while squirreling money away for vacations and unexpected expenses.

"She worked so hard and took care of anything," said Shirley Yohman, who lived next door to the Priakos with her husband, Henry, and was close with Helen. "She was the matriarch of that house."

Like Bill, Helen lived for her children, but not through them. She made her own desserts, making sure they had one every night at dinner. Helen, being Helen, once took a cake decorating class so she could make Bill and the kids' birthdays extra special.

"My mom didn't go to college, but she was one of the smartest people I know," said Kathy Sekera, the youngest of the Priatko children. "She had so much common sense and so much practicality and was just very intuitive. She was a great listener. She was a very, very hard worker. She never stopped."

Nothing better illustrated Helen's can-do spirit than the kids' annual back-to-school shopping trip. Since Helen couldn't drive, she and the four kids walked a mile to the nearest bus stop. They hopped a bus and rode to Greengate Mall in Greensburg. She made sure each child had what they needed for school and indulged them whenever possible.

"We grew up not deprived of anything," said Debbie, the oldest of the children. "It was kind of like *Leave It to Beaver,* but my dad was a disciplinarian. He made us toe the line. He wanted us to do the right thing, always uphold the family name."

Bill always emphasized to his children that when you do good, good things come of it. And when you do bad, bad things come of it. It sounded simple but teenage angst and the tug of rebellion have a way of making life more complicated than that. Yet the people who taught and coached the Priatko children found them to be reflections of what Bill told them.

"The way that Dan was on the field, and even off the field, he just had so many traits that as a parent you would be so proud of," said Al Lynn, who coached Dan and David in football at Norwin. "More and more, as I got to know them with Dave coming up, the virtues that they had, the traits that they had are from the two great role models they have in their lives."

"Dan was the guy who would never bring embarrassment to his family," said his Norwin classmate and friend, Kevin Donnelly, "and never bring embarrassment to himself."

The closest he may have come to doing that involved his sports rooting interests.

Geography and the fact that his father had played for the Steelers didn't resonate with Dan when he was young. A team with flashy stars on the sides of its helmets did. So did its swashbuckling quarterback Roger Staubach.

"My friend and I were die-hard Dallas fans," Dan admitted, a tad sheepishly, years later. "That was before the Steelers started to win."

The Steelers, long defined by futility that was exacerbated by blunders such as cutting Johnny Unitas, started to win big in the early 1970s, not long after Chuck Noll took over as head coach.

The Steelers flipped Dan's allegiance as they transformed themselves into the NFL's team of the decade. He was one of eight family members who piled into an uncle's motorhome for a drive to New Orleans after the Steelers made the 1974 Super Bowl. Bill got eight tickets from Leon Hart, who was president of the NFL Alumni Association and an old friend and rival from Turtle Creek High School. Bill sent him a $120 check for the eight tickets, a sign of the times that Super Bowl tickets were that inexpensive.

What was priceless was something that happened before the Steelers' 1978 Super Bowl appearance in Miami. Noll had given Bill passes to watch the Steelers' final practice. Dan and David went with him. Debbie stayed behind and promptly made herself comfortable on the hood of a car owned by a young defensive back named Tony Dungy. Outside of the Orange Bowl, an *Associated Press* photographer spotted Debbie reading a Harlequin romance novel. He snapped a picture of her, before Dungy emerged from practice and yelled, "Who is that sitting on my car?"

Newspapers all over the county ran the photo the day of the Super Bowl, including the Greensburg *Tribune-Review*, the Priatkos' hometown newspaper. Debbie, being a teenager, grumbled that she had not been able to properly do her hair since they were staying in a neighbor's motorhome. Decades later, after Dungy became a successful NFL coach (he made history in 2007 when he became the first African-American head coach to win the Super Bowl), he and Bill laughed at the memory of Bill's first-born child turning the hood of Dungy's car into a reading lounge.

David and Dan posed with defensive back Tony Dungy in the Steelers' final practice before the 1978 Super Bowl, but it was the *Associated Press* photo of Debbie on the hood of Dungy's car that appeared in newspapers across the country.

Memories the Priatkos created over trips to the Super Bowls and family vacations made for idyllic childhoods for the four kids. And it had nothing to do with the make of their TV, the model of their car, or the cost of their clothes.

"There were times when things were tight and we didn't even know it," David said. "We were blessed to have the upbringing that we did. We were raised to have good values and a good work ethic as well."

They were also raised to have inner strength and toughness. It came from faith and the examples they saw at home.

Dan embodied those traits.

So did his mother.

Of the four Priatko children, Dan may have taken the most after his mother in terms of demeanor. Helen possessed a preternatural calm and sweetness about her, as did Dan. But Dan and Helen's outward appearance masked a fierce determination. Dan's accident brought it to the surface in each of them.

From the time he survived the accident, Dan continually defied odds. In the years that followed, he did just about everything doctors said he would not or might not be able to do, except make a full recovery. And Dan *never* accepted that he wouldn't make a full recovery.

Meanwhile, Helen never buckled under the enormous pressure she was under during Dan's recovery. Her positivity rarely wavered; her demeanor never did. When she was diagnosed with bladder cancer and given the worst possible prognosis, Bill didn't need to hand her a tissue after they left the urologist's office.

Helen refused to believe it. She simply wouldn't accept leaving Dan when he still needed her. It is impossible to quantify how much her will and fierce maternal instincts helped her fight cancer.

Her urologist, Dr. James McCague, likened it to a parent doing something superhuman such as lifting a car off their child. It should not be physiologically possible, but it has been done. In Helen's case, she did that heavy lifting for almost three decades for Dan. She endured chemotherapy treatments, even a second mastectomy through the years, but never blinked.

"Mrs. Priatko was a remarkably devoted, focused woman," McCague said. "And she had plans; she had demands that she was going to pursue and she was not going to change them."

It is fitting that, while Helen never served in the military, her doctor saw in her approach to battling cancer the never-give-up mentality that Dan demonstrated in his recovery from the car accident.

"There is a very hard to analyze military element in some people, a real devotion, a real self-sacrifice, an intrepidness, and I always thought she had that," McCague said. "There was no long-suffering quality about her at all. She was dealing with problems as they came. Nothing lingered with that woman. She moved from therapy to the next thing. She moved from one diagnosis to the next thing. She was just a terrific lady."

Helen received plenty of prayers along the way.

It was not uncommon for former Steelers offensive lineman Tunch Ilkin, a devout Christian, to call Helen so they could pray together. That always left Helen smiling — "It warms my heart," she would tell Bill of Ilkin's support — but then she always seemed to be smiling.

"You'd never know she was sick," said Dr. Philip Dahar, an orthodontist and close family friend. "She was always happy, always jovial."

It was even that way behind closed doors.

"She would never let on that she wasn't feeling well," Debbie said. "She was a little woman, but boy, was she a fighter. There aren't enough words to describe her."

One night, Helen was so sick that she spent the night on the couch so she wouldn't keep Bill awake. She barely slept, yet first thing in the morning she went to Dan and asked if *he* needed anything.

"That's my mom," Dan said, "always thinking of others."

Dan and Helen celebrate Dan's birthday.

Dan couldn't count the number of times he brought home football uniforms covered with mud or grass stains. Helen always washed them for him without complaint. She did the same when Dan returned home from West Point with a bag full of dirty laundry. The most she might say was, "Ah, Dan, what am I going to do with you?" And she almost always said it with a smile.

Bill adored the woman he fell in love with for the wife and mother she became. She did everything in his eyes. That included saving his life. One time, a wicked thunderstorm rolled through western Pennsylvania and toppled a tree in the Priatkos' front yard. Bill went out to inspect and didn't think a wire that the tree had taken down was live. He was less than a foot from it when Helen intuitively shouted, "Stop!"

Later, as a technician repaired the damaged lines, Bill asked if the line he almost touched had indeed been live.

"That was as live as live can be," the technician said. "You were lucky."

All because of Helen.

"She was my saint," Bill said.

In every possible way.

Chapter V

THE LONG GRAY LINE

B ill and Dan were at Cameron Indoor Stadium at Duke University for a men's college basketball game when two hands pushed down on Bill's shoulders. He turned around and saw the smiling, square-jawed face of former Pittsburgh Steelers coach Bill Cowher. Cowher, long retired from coaching, was taking in the North Carolina-Duke game with one of his daughters.

"What are you doing here?" Bill said. "Your alma mater's playing right down the road tonight."

Cowher, a North Carolina State graduate, pointed to the ground to indicate that *this* was the place to be. With Dan and Bill seated right behind Duke's bench, Cowher could have been forgiven if he had asked, "What are *you* doing here?"

By the time of that chance encounter with Cowher, Dan and Bill had forged a unique friendship with Blue Devils coach Mike Krzyzewski. Their seats—Krzyzewski always made sure Dan and Bill were behind his team's bench and often shared a look with Dan after the National Anthem—weren't the only token of that friendship.

Bill has an overflowing manila folder with letters and emails from Krzyzewski. One of the pictures hanging in the Priatko game room shows "Coach K" and Dan standing side by side and smiling.

Krzyzewski autographed the picture: "To Dan: Thanks For Being My Special Friend! Go Army!!"

Krzyzewski's reverence for Army is well-documented. He played basketball at West Point and started his coaching career there. He initially liked West Point about as much as a root canal and wanted to get as far away from it as possible. His dad wouldn't hear any talk of quitting when Krzyzewski returned home to Chicago his freshman year for Christmas break. He reluctantly returned to West Point and eventually thrived there before graduating in 1969. Krzyzewski, men's college basketball's all-winningest coach, has said staying at West Point is one of the best things he ever did.

That is why he took such an interest in Bill after they first met, and Krzyzewski sensed that Bill knew a thing or two about West Point. Their paths crossed again almost nine months later in Atlanta. Robert Morris University made the 1990 NCAA men's basketball tournament and found itself in the same region as Duke.

Bill traveled with the team to Atlanta for its first-round game against mighty Kansas. He had a letter that Dan had given to him for Krzyzewski. Bill told Dan he would do his best to get the letter to Krzyzewski. But, even if he got close enough at the cavernous Omni Coliseum, would Krzyzewski even remember him?

Bill watched Duke win its first-round game of the tournament with ease. Shortly after Duke beat Richmond, Krzyzewski was walking to his post-game press conference, right past where Bill had strategically positioned himself.

Bill called his name. To his surprise, Krzyzewski turned around and said, "Bill, how's Dan?" Bill handed him Dan's letter, and Krzyzewski saluted before walking away. Krzyzewski later wrote to Dan how much he appreciated the letter. In the note that came with a package of Duke basketball paraphernalia, Krzyzewski told Dan that if his players had his "competitive spirit," Duke would win the national championship every year.

Dan and Krzyzewski met for the first time a couple of months later when "Coach K" returned to the Five-Star Basketball Camp.

"Dan," Krzyzewski said after hugging him, "we have that bond. We were on that Long Gray Line together."

Krzyzewski and the Priatkos stayed in regular contact after that meeting. Bill and Dan attended their first game at Cameron Indoor Stadium in 1993, the season after Duke had won its second-straight national championship. It was the start of an annual trip that continues to this day.

The first year Bill tried to pay for the tickets. Gerry Brown, Krzyzewski's longtime administrative assistant, told Bill she couldn't accept any money because there were no available tickets for the sold-out game.

In other words, his money was no good there.

Dan with iconic TV college basketball analyst Dick Vitale at a Duke game at Cameron Indoor Stadium

During subsequent visits to Duke, Krzyzewski always took time to meet with Dan and Bill. He told them that his mother had been born in Keisterville, a tiny hamlet in southwestern Pennsylvania near Uniontown. She lived there until moving to Chicago as a young girl; Krzyzewski had visited the area for family reunions. He loved it because of the people and how it had molded his mother.

Dan told Krzyzewski about Cameron Indoor Stadium's Norwin connection. The gym had been named after former Blue Devils athletic director Edward Cameron, who, like Dan, was a Norwin graduate.

One time, Bill wanted to do something for Krzyzewski to show his appreciation. A friend of his was going to Poland for vacation so Bill asked him to get something in Krakow where Krzyzewski's father was from. He bought a blue crystal in Duke's colors, and Bill sent it to Krzyzewski. It ended up on the mantel in the Krzyzewski living room – "Every time I look at the vase I think of my dad," Krzyzewski once told Dan and Bill – symbolizing the strong friendship between Krzyzewski and the Priatkos.

"Dan, thanks for being my good friend," Krzyzewski once wrote. "I surely hope that you will be able to come and see us play this season. You are an amazing family, and getting to know you as well as I have has been one of the truly enjoyable parts of my life."

Dan reciprocated that sentiment in a letter he wrote to Krzyzewski:

Dear Coach K,

As we know at West Point, we learned about performing "above and beyond the call of duty." Your life is a true example of that concept! Thank you so much for all of your kindness to me, including your speaking with me at Robert Morris University. Your kind words about me in the introduction to your presentation are also greatly appreciated. And the way you signed the picture is especially meaningful coming from a man of your character!

That character had to have left a positive impression with the young men. As we also know, the example we set is the most effective way of teaching. Your true class and professionalism impact all you come in contact with. Your background as a member of and coaching the Long Gray Line is evident in your conduct.

Again, Coach K, I am truly appreciative of your thoughtfulness! As we celebrate the Bicentennial of the United States Military Academy, you are to be commended for living its motto of "Duty, Honor, Country." With a high sense of duty, you serve basketball and mankind, you do so living and teaching honor, and you serve our country by trying to instill in young people character and pride. May God bless you peace, health, and strength as you continue your fine work!

With gratitude, respect, and friendship,
Dan Priatko
P.S. On Brave Old Army Team!
P.P.S. Go Duke!

Winning five national championships and three Olympics gold medals has made Krzyzewski one of the all-time greatest basketball coaches at any level. But he is a friend first to Dan, a fellow West

Pointer with whom he shares a bond because of their shared experiences and ideals.

"I had more of an appreciation after my accident for sincerity and genuine intentions, and I saw that in him," Dan said. "I can tell what a person means by what they say and do. The whole country should know what type of man Coach K is."

Duke men's basketball coach Mike Krzyzewski with Dan and Bill at Five-Star Basketball Camp at Robert Morris University

To Bill, the friendship with Krzyzewski always comes back to the Long Gray Line, the three words that bond all West Pointers in ways they can only understand.

"He never forgets Dan," Bill said.

Neither does West Point.

Art Gerometta played on one of college football's all-time greatest teams in 1945.

Army rolled to a 9-0 record, outscoring opponents 412-46 on the way to an undisputed national championship. Army beat eight of its opponents by at least twenty-one points and seven of its opponents by at least thirty-two points.

Gerometta played guard, earning All-American honors that season while blocking for the unstoppable running back duo of Doc Blanchard and Glenn Davis (the former won the Heisman Trophy in 1945, the latter won college football's highest honor the following season).

Gerometta returned to West Point in the fall of 1990 as a revered figure because of his exploits on both the football field and battlefield. Army was celebrating its 100th season of football, and one of the memories that stayed with Gerometta was meeting Dan Priatko.

Dan joined former Black Knights football players for the celebration, five and a half years after his accident. Dan had willed himself to walk again, but he still used a wheelchair when he was somewhere that required a lot of walking or standing. Dan's mere presence at the 100th-year anniversary inspired Gerometta. When the two met, Gerometta hugged him and said, "Dan, you're one of us. You came into Michie Stadium just like we did."

Dan and former All-American guard Art Gerometta at the 100th celebration
of Army football in 1990

Dan stood with Gerometta and other former West Point football players on The Plain while the Army Glee Club sang the alma mater. Before Army's game against Rutgers University, Gerometta pushed Dan in his wheelchair onto the field. Later, at a reception, this toughest of tough guys hugged Dan again and said, "I'll never forget you."

Two weeks later, a package arrived at the Priatko household from Gerometta. It included the Purple Heart and Silver Star awards that he earned while serving in Korea. There was also a letter in which Gerometta wrote to Dan, "You are the epitome of courage." Gerometta's gesture was another example of how West Point continued to rally around Dan.

In 1995, five years after the celebration of Army's 100th football season, Dan returned to West Point to speak to the cadets.

Anyone who was inside the Gothic cathedral a couple of days before Thanksgiving would never forget it.

Dan walked slowly to the podium, declining any assistance until he got to the microphone. Nate Sassaman, the starting quarterback Dan's senior season at Army, took his former teammate by the arm and helped him to the podium. The two had not seen each other since Dan had graduated from West Point, but they were forever linked by the Long Gray Line.

What follows is an abridged version of what Dan said to more than 700 cadets and others in the church:

"In the dictionary, Thanksgiving is defined as an expression of gratitude, especially to God. God has used adversity in my life to make me more thankful for everything that I do have. During my days here at the Academy, I knew the significance of right and wrong in our cadet relationships through the Cadet Honor Code. More than ever, I am grateful that I have gained, through my accident, the strength our Lord has given me.

I am thankful for my upbringing, to include my family life, the high school I attended, and a father and mother who raised me in a God-fearing home. I am so grateful I came to West Point to be part of the Long Gray Line. I am thankful for the mental and physical disciplines that were instilled in me. I drew upon these quite often during my battle to win back my abilities to walk and talk, and other rehabilitation efforts. What compels me to do more of an exercise than I have been instructed to do is the instinct to go above and beyond the call of duty. When fatigue would try to take over, making it easier to alibi, I remembered the words from the Cadet Prayer of choosing the harder right over the easier wrong.

My gratitude extends to the years I spent as an Army football player. The perseverance that I learned helped me so much in adapting to a changed lifestyle over the past ten years. I was often motivated by the words of Coach Jim Young when he said, 'What the mind can conceive, the body can achieve.' I am very thankful to be speaking here tonight in the Cadet Chapel. I am so appreciative for the spiritual training I received here during my years at the Academy and the leadership and support provided by Chaplain Camp and his staff. The spiritual training has continued to be a great help to me since those days."

Cadets shot up in the pews and clapped after Dan had finished speaking. When the applause started to wane, it started up again. It did not stop until Dan had returned to his seat. The thunderous ovation lasted close to ten minutes, leading to an outbreak of goosebumps.

The surreal scene stirred something in Kathy Camp. Camp's father was Chaplain Richard Camp, a motorcycle-riding, marathon-running man of God with whom Dan had become close while at West Point. Nearly two decades after Dan's speech, Camp could still see the scene like it was yesterday.

"You had these nineteen-year-old alpha male cadets in their stark uniforms leaning forward to grasp every word that he said," she recalled.

After the service, Dan and Bill went to dinner at Chaplain Camp's house. As they were sitting around the dining room table, Camp told Dan that he was only the fourth person he had invited to speak at the Thanksgiving service. The other three had been a Catholic Church Cardinal, the leading rabbi in the nation and a U.S. Senator. "Dan," Camp told him, "you were the best."

Dan stayed in touch with the Camp family. Kathy always marveled at what he wrote. The elegance of it amazed her as did Dan's attitude. His positivity helped Camp and her family when her father started slipping because of Parkinson's disease.

Bill and Dan with former West Point chaplain Richard Camp and his wife, Virjean, at an Army football game. Reverend Camp was recruited to play football at Army by the legendary Vince Lombardi. He chose the ministry over football but later ended up at West Point and became a revered figure there.

"For somebody that has every reason to be glass half empty, for every reason to be angry at God, angry at the world, angry at the circumstances, he's the opposite," Camp said. "He really has been a great support for my family and what we're going through despite all the challenges he goes through, and I think that's what makes him remarkable. He's been given this otherworldly aptitude for hope that defies our earthly logic. His capacity for hope and love is not something that can make sense logically in this world."

B ill's days with the Cleveland Browns created lasting and cherished friendships with Chuck Noll and Dick LeBeau. Both of those friendships developed into close ones after Noll and later LeBeau started coaching in Pittsburgh.

Noll arrived in 1969 as a little-known assistant coach. He was charged with no less than changing the culture of an organization that had been tagged with the pejorative moniker "Same Old Steelers." Noll won his head-coaching debut—and then lost the last thirteen games of the season. But he stayed the course and transformed the Steelers. Noll led them to four Super Bowl titles in the 1970s, while Bill had a pretty good seat for that historic run. Noll invited him and family members to watch the final practice before every one of those Super Bowls. Any time Bill went to St. Vincent College in Latrobe for training camp, he was allowed on the practice fields. Afterward, he and Noll would walk up the hill that overlooks the fields, talking just like they had at Browns' training camp as teammates.

Steelers coach Chuck Noll with Dan and David during the team's final practice before the 1978 Super Bowl

When Noll retired after the 1991 season, the Steelers hired Bill Cowher. Among the assistants he brought to Pittsburgh was defensive backs coach Dick LeBeau, Bill's onetime training camp roommate.

LeBeau and Bill renewed their friendship, eventually becoming the closest of friends. LeBeau established himself as one of the most esteemed defensive coordinators in the NFL during two stints with the Steelers and was hailed as an innovator with his zone blitzes. He and Bill talked and met regularly. They ate lunch together once a week during the season at the Steelers' practice facility. One thing that LeBeau learned from spending time with Bill is that Bill knows *everybody* in the Pittsburgh area.

Or at least seems to know everybody.

"Anywhere I ever went with him, fifty people knew him," LeBeau said, laughing. "Or if he doesn't, within thirty seconds (of meeting), they'll be bonded brothers."

Bill doesn't have a group of friends; he has a galaxy of them.

His mother always told him to be nice to people. He goes beyond that. Bill is an inveterate letter writer and card sender. His kids always joke that they should buy him stamps for his birthday. His generosity with people is surpassed only by how genuine he is.

Bill's visibility in western Pennsylvania brought a lot of attention to Dan's plight. It also generated support from a Who's Who of area sports figures.

Steelers founder and owner, Art Rooney, wrote to Dan regularly after Dan's accident. His son, Art Rooney Jr., continues the tradition that "The Chief," who passed away in 1988, started. Rooney Jr. still writes to Dan once a week. It doesn't matter if he is on vacation, or even overseas.

"He's just a special, special guy," Rooney Jr. said.

Art Rooney Jr., who helped build the Steelers teams that won four Super
Bowls in the 1970s, and Dan at the Pennsylvania Sports Hall of Fame dinner
in 2017 for Rooney's induction

Joe Paterno thought so, too. The legendary Penn State football
coach and Bill got to know each other through football and became
friends. When Paterno wrote to Bill, he always ended letters by giving
his best to Dan. One year, Paterno attended a dinner honoring former
Penn State and Steelers great Dick Hoak. Held at the Sheraton Hotel
in Greensburg, it was a big deal for local Penn State alumni.

Some became impatient before dinner as they waited to get a picture with Paterno or an autograph. More than a few had to ask themselves, *Who is that with Joe?* It was Dan, and Paterno spent more than
forty minutes chatting with him in a hospitality room. He might have
kept on talking had a bell not rung signaling the start of dinner.

"He told me, 'God has a purpose for you,'" Dan said.

The emcee of that dinner could also be counted among the
famous sports figures who were well aware of Dan. Legendary Steelers

broadcaster, Myron Cope, always asked Bill about Dan, never failing to add, "I root for that kid."

People, such as Cope, the inventor of the "Terrible Towel," no doubt rooted for Dan because of their association with Bill. But Dan also made it easy for them because of how he handled his situation. He never complained, never asked why. To this day, Dan's stock answer whenever asked how he is doing is "wonderful." Bill will joke with him, telling him that no one can feel wonderful every single day. But that is Dan.

"If that happened to me," Rooney Jr. said of Dan's accident, "I would be screaming like every third minute, 'What did I do to deserve this?' I have such a great admiration of him being a soldier and going through that special training. He probably would have been a tremendous combat (soldier). He's almost like something out of a movie."

Dorothy Tragesser wouldn't argue with that. She worked with Dan as his speech therapist and couldn't believe the progress he made before they started worked together. She *still* finds it hard to believe what he has accomplished when looking at it through the lens of her professional experience.

"Most people who have been in a coma as long as he was would not have been able to do anything. Nothing," she said. "His walking is not functional. It really isn't. Most people would have just gotten in a wheelchair after that and been done with it. Never, ever did I hear a negative word. He just always was moving forward, like with his walking."

Not walking again was never a consideration for Dan. He spent countless hours working on it in the hallways of Norwin High School or on the school's football field. His accident robbed Dan of so much. The one thing he refused to let it take was his essence.

That explains why he addressed the visiting Jacksonville Jaguars before they played the Steelers in 1996. Vic Ketchman had been the longtime sports editor of the Irwin *Standard Observer* before taking a job writing for the Jaguars. He arranged for Dan to speak to the team during its chapel service the night before the game. Here is part of Dan's speech:

"As the reality of my accident settled in, I faced a choice. I could become bitter and depressed, wondering, 'Why me?' Or I could live each day to the best of my ability, trusting in Jesus Christ to be my source of peace and strength. Fortunately, I chose trusting in the Lord... And to you, I will express the same thought, and will also state with all sincerity that my accident has brought me closer to Christ. I was fortunate, and you have the opportunity to play the greatest game in the world—football. No other game reflects life the way football does. The values we learn from football can help us in life. We sometimes experience the agony of defeat, and few emotions can equal the elation of victory. As in life, we have to rebound after a defeat and face tomorrow. In your case, facing a new tomorrow is mentally and physically preparing to meet a new opponent in the following week. The mental toughness so essential in football is also integral in leading a successful life."

After his speech, Dan told the Jaguars, "Now I want you guys to be successful but not tomorrow. You're playing my Steelers."

Apparently, there was no offense taken.

Jaguars quarterback Mark Brunell hugged Dan and thanked him. Coach Tom Coughlin told Dan how inspirational his talk had been, the part about the Steelers notwithstanding.

The Steelers beat the Jaguars, 28-3, the next day at Heinz Field. The loss seemingly dropped Jacksonville out of postseason contention, but they won their next five games to sneak into the playoffs.

The Jaguars upset the Buffalo Bills in the wild-card round. Then they stunned the Broncos in Denver to make the AFC Championship Game in just the franchise's second season. Jacksonville's magical run ended the next week in New England with a loss to the Patriots.

A little-known footnote to that season is that the Jaguars went 7-2 after Dan's speech.

They had been 4-7 before it.

R inggold High School, thirty miles south of Pittsburgh, is most famous for being the alma mater of Joe Montana. It can also lay claim to St. Louis Cardinals immortal Stan Musial. "Stan the Man" went to Donora High School, as did Ken Griffey, Sr., before it merged with Monongahela High School to form Ringgold.

Still in its glory days as the 1980s headed into the fourth quarter, Ringgold lost just one game in 1987 and made a run at a Western Pennsylvania Interscholastic Athletic League (WPIAL) title. That is when Ringgold coach Joe Ravasio first met Dan. He had learned about him from school athletics director Paul Zolak, who attended the same church in Donora as the Priatkos and was the father of Scott Zolak, arguably the second-best quarterback in Ringgold history.

Every Thursday night during the season, Ravasio invited someone to speak to his players about football and life. Dan addressed them less than two years after his accident.

"Out of all the speakers that we brought in, and the others were very, very good, none of them captured their attention, their emotions, their thought process the way Danny Priatko did," Ravasio said. "I can still hear his words: 'Cherish that moment. Love that guy next to you.' From that time on, Danny and Bill became like family."

No one sat more rapt as Dan spoke to Ringgold's football team than running back/linebacker Marcus McCullough. The senior captain was the blood and guts of the team, an unquestioned leader who searched for inspiration anywhere he could find it. That night, in the music room at Ringgold High School, McCullough listened as Dan talked about his accident and the power of perseverance. What made McCullough really sit up was when Dan said, "You have to overcome who you are to get to where you have to be."

"How I took that (was) if you don't overcome who you are," McCullough said, "you're never going to be anything greater than what you are."

He needed that approach after tearing his anterior cruciate ligament (ACL) late in the season. McCullough returned for the Rams' first playoff game and played on essentially one leg. McCullough played the following week, too, in a close loss that ended Ringgold's season.

McCullough had received some Division I interest during his senior season, but the knee injury effectively ended his playing career. He went into coaching at the age of twenty-one and joined Ravasio's staff. He has spent almost three decades coaching at numerous schools in western Pennsylvania. McCullough has never forgotten Dan's speech at Ringgold. He still credits Dan for helping him battle through the knee injury in his final football season.

"There's no doubt about it because I'm the type of person who's very consistent about listening to people who are very positive," McCullough said. "If they're giving me a lesson, I'm listening. That guy, he struck me. He had a commanding presence."

More than a decade after speaking at Ringgold, Dan's inspirational presence resonated at his alma mater.

Norwin football coach Tim McCabe had known the Priatkos for years and experienced firsthand the uplifting power of Dan. The simple act of getting out of a car was a struggle for Dan, but he never quit, never accepted help. McCabe had seen this and tapped into Dan's ability to inspire through sheer grit. He invited Dan to speak to his team prior to the 2000 season.

One speech turned into another and another. Before the end of the season, Norwin had given Dan his own jersey, making him a ceremonial part of the team.

"Just to hear him talk and see what he went through and see how tough as nails he is, the kids really related to that," McCabe said. "Many times when he spoke, there wasn't a dry eye in the locker room, and the kids went out and played to a different level."

That season the Knights made the playoffs with a team that had only ten seniors and been an afterthought to preseason prognosticators. They reached the WPIAL Championship game for the first time in school history, and Dan was with them every step of the way.

The signature moment for Dan and those Knights came in a close win against Ringgold. Norwin fumbled late in the game, giving Ringgold the ball deep in Knights' territory. Ringgold made a first down just inside the 5-yard line and was poised to win with a touchdown.

Before the game, Dan had talked about being an Army Ranger and how "Rangers never quit." He told the players to remember that if they needed to make a goal-line stand.

They remembered.

Norwin stopped Ringgold short of the end zone on four consecutive plays. The win defined their season and Dan's impact on them.

"A lot of kids after the game referenced Danny's pre-game speech, how you never give up, no matter how bad things look, and you never, ever feel sorry for yourself," McCabe said. "They really believed in what he was saying."

That team was a perfect reflection of Dan. Like Dan when he had played at Norwin, the Knights were greater than the sum of their parts. And like Dan after suffering a debilitating tragedy, the notion of giving in when circumstances conspired against them was simply unacceptable.

"They were truly a band of brothers," McCabe said. "They believed in themselves and worked really hard. When Dan was done talking to them, they would feed off what he said. They would be shouting it in the locker room, shouting it on the way to the field."

F rom calling orders to an Army battalion to calling Bingo games is how Dan sometimes frames the accident that changed his life. He does so with a laugh, putting others at ease, and never with a hint of bitterness. That is one reason why Dan Wukich grew to love him like a son.

Wukich grew up in North Braddock on the same street as Bill. He was ten years younger than Bill and had idolized him. Years later, Wukich met Dan during a chance encounter and learned he was Bill's son.

"I just hit it off with him," Wukich said. "I can't explain it."

Wukich owns Loyalhanna Care Center in Latrobe, Pennsylvania, and he told the manager to create a position for Dan as a part-time recreation aide. Wukich hired Dan for $5,000 a year. Dan, of course, approached the job as if he was getting paid six figures.

He played cards with residents and prayed with those who needed it. He called numbers for Bingo games, something Wukich couldn't believe anyone volunteered to do since the players could be as cutthroat as they were impatient. Dan loved it.

Dan quickly fell into an easy give and take with those at Loyalhanna, including his boss. Dan used a motorized wheelchair to make his rounds. Wukich never failed to feign outrage over Dan recharging the wheelchair on days that he didn't work.

"You know Pratko," Wukich would say, calling Dan the nickname his father had in North Braddock, "if you don't start paying me for that electricity, I'm going to have to get rid of you."

Dan always laughed and gave as good as he got.

Before the annual Army-Navy football games, he posted "Go Army!" signs all over the nursing home. Wukich told Dan to also put up Navy signs in the interest of fairness. That was apparently one of the few exceptions that Dan allowed himself for rank insubordination.

"He would laugh, and of course he would ignore me," Wukich said. "He has a great sense of humor. He used his affliction to create happiness and relationships with individuals. He wasn't asking for pity. He was just waiting for me to holler about him using my electricity. He would expect no less from me. People couldn't wait for him to show up in their room to play cards or whatever he was there to do."

Dan in separate pictures with all three of Army's Heisman Trophy winners: Pete Dawkins (tuxedo), Glenn "Mr. Outside" Davis, and Doc "Mr. Inside" Blanchard

What impressed Wukich most was how Dan spent time with those who were near the end.

"Here's a guy with the kind of problems he has, and he's trying to console them and helping them meet their Maker," Wukich said. "I couldn't do that. His character, his demeanor was always positive. Always."

Dan worked for twenty years at Loyalhanna. He reluctantly left for a volunteer job at another senior care facility, Redstone Highlands in North Huntingdon, because it was closer to home. Wukich was crushed but he understood. He was thankful that Dan had helped so many people during his time at Loyalhanna. And that Dan had helped make him a better man.

"Danny is one of the most unforgettable people I'll ever meet," Wukich said. "In my life, I've made a couple of good decisions. (Hiring Dan) has to be at the top of the list. It has made my life a heck of a lot better."

E van Offstein graduated from West Point in 1994, a decade after Dan. Like Dan, he hails from western Pennsylvania and has been shaped by his roots and West Point experience.

He wrote a book on his experience, *Stand Your Ground: Building Honorable Leaders the West Point Way*. Norwin superintendent Dr. William Kerr, after hearing Offstein speak, thought the book would be the perfect complement to the award Dan received on March 20, 2017. That day, Kerr presented him with the first Noble Knight Award, which recognizes Norwin graduates who exemplify character traits that include courage, perseverance, and caring. Offstein sent an autographed copy of the book to Dan.

Two weeks prior to the Noble Knight Award presentation, Offstein and Dan had become linked by more than West Point and western Pennsylvania. Offstein's daughter, Molly, was hit by a truck while jogging one morning at Elon College in North Carolina and was almost killed.

Where Offstein and Molly's story mirror that of Dan's is how West Point rallied around his family in its greatest hour of need.

When Offstein arrived at University of North Carolina Hospital in Chapel Hill, a fellow cadet that he had not talked to since graduation was waiting for him. He took Offstein's keys and parked the car so Offstein could go to Molly right away. Other cadets booked him and his fiancée a room at a hotel and took care of other logistical items, allowing Offstein to focus on Molly. A GoFundMe account was started for Molly. Word of it traveled through the West Point community at warp speed. The goal was to raise $20,000 in thirty days; double was raised in six days.

That response is almost like a reflex for West Pointers. It puts into context why Mike Krzyzewski insisted on meeting Dan right away after hearing Dan's story. That is simply what West Pointers do for one another, especially in times of need. That is also why Krzyzewski shrugs off any notion that he did something special that day or in his ongoing friendship with Dan and Bill.

"It's a fellow West Pointer, and someone who is facing incredible adversity," Krzyzewski said. "I thought it was something a West Pointer should do for another West Pointer. We share the same oath, and our oath is to have a lifetime of service to our country, whether it be in the military or civilian life. When you take the same oath as somebody, there's a bond there."

Long Gray Line and DUTY-HONOR-COUNTRY, as displayed on the West Point crest, tie all United States Military Academy graduates together. Photo courtesy of United States Military Academy.

The bond can be distilled to three words: Long Gray Line.

It links all West Point graduates because of experiences that are unique to most schools. Adversity is built into academy life, and it starts from the moment they step onto campus.

"You are tested physically, academically, militarily, and you fail at something every day at West Point," said Offstein, whose brother is also an Army graduate. "You have to learn to get up and rely on friends to help."

The camaraderie this fosters manifests itself long after cadets leave West Point. It did with Dan. It did with Offstein, and it doesn't take a tragedy to bring it out.

Andrew Glen, a classmate of Dan's at West Point, said he could drive across the country and never spend money on a hotel. West Pointers along the way would insist that he and his wife stay with them. Even if they had never met, they know each other because of West Point.

"I may keep in touch with one person from my high school, but we send out 200 Christmas cards a year," Glen said. "The vast majority of them are probably West Pointers."

Dan with Army classmate and close friend Dr. Andrew Glen at
West Point

If a bond exists among West Pointers who have never met, imagine the bond among those who went through West Point together. Glen has that with Dan, which means the two could go years without contact and then pick right back up as friends. Brothers, even.

"Some people you lose your friendship with, but not with Dan and people like that," Glen said. "You know each other. It's like we never said goodbye."

Dan feels the same way about West Point. He and Bill return every football season for a game, and West Point has also come to Dan.

Three times the West Point Glee Club performed at Norwin High School in honor of Dan. The school auditorium was packed every time and became a community event. Cadets stayed with host families, giving those individuals a glimpse into what makes West Point special.

"Everyone who housed a cadet said it was one of the greatest experiences of their life," Bill said.

Seeing one of the performances is an experience that Joe Mucci, one of Bill's good friends, will never forget.

Mucci won almost 189 games, against just forty-nine losses, during a legendary prep football coaching career in western Pennsylvania. He attended one of the programs with his son, a Naval Academy graduate. The Glee Club's pomp and precision awed Mucci. So did the respect it showed by singing hymns associated with the other military academies. What impressed Mucci most is what happened after Dan was called to the stage to sing the West Point alma mater with the Glee Club.

"People wanted to help him, and he absolutely refused it," Mucci said. "He wanted to walk up to the gentleman who was at that microphone, and he made it up there. That was one of the most powerful things."

It got even better.

Taking the microphone, the Glee Club leader said, "We are going to dedicate the next song to Dan Priatko, and we will dedicate this song at every future concert we perform in the United States and explain his story to the audience. It is called 'Soldiers Again.'"

The song is about a young boy who dreams of becoming a soldier. Life events prevent him from becoming one but, according to the song, he becomes a soldier again in the Army of the Lord. The audience gave a standing ovation after the Glee Club sang the song. It left some people in tears.

The Glee Club kept its promise, too. Bill received proof of that a year later after getting a phone call from Dan's aunt, Anita Pollick. She and her daughter, Pam, had attended an Army Glee Club performance at a central Pennsylvania high school. They sang "Soldiers Again" in honor of Dan and told the audience Dan's story.

Dan with his aunt, Anita Pollick

Dan Wukich never made it to one of the Army Glee Club performances. Several of his employees went and told him how incredible they were.

It wasn't that Wukich was too busy to go or didn't want to attend. He *couldn't* go.

He knew seeing "Pratko," as he has always called Dan, in that setting would turn him into a quivering mess. He knew there was no way he would be able to keep it together.

Chapter VI

KEEPING THE FAITH

G reg Petrick and Dan Priatko met in junior high school and developed a close friendship. They pushed each academically and athletically. Petrick credits Dan with helping him achieve a dream by receiving an appointment to the Air Force Academy.

That is not the most meaningful thing he gained from their decades-long friendship.

"Dan Priatko played an instrumental role in my giving my life to Jesus and becoming a Christian," Petrick said.

That pivotal moment occurred after their sophomore year at Norwin. Dan invited Petrick to a Fellowship of Christian Athletes football camp. Petrick had been raised in a nominal Christian home, but he questioned God's existence. Part of the reason he attended the FCA camp is because he saw a strong faith and correlating sense of self in Dan.

"Plus, we were friends and he wanted to invite me to share something that was important to him," Petrick said. "That's basic evangelism."

Petrick's path to Christianity reflects how religion was at the foundation of Dan's life long before his accident. Dan and his siblings grew up in St. Nicholas Orthodox Church in Donora. The family almost never missed church. During the holiest period of the year, they attended services on Holy Thursday, twice on Good Friday, and on Easter.

To Bill and Helen, religion extended beyond the confines of the church. Each regularly read the Bible and followed a Christian lifestyle. Their example may have been the greatest gift that they passed down to their children.

Dan stayed true to his beliefs at West Point, and religion was a big part of his college experience. He found mentors in West Point Chaplain Richard Camp and Major Albert Sleder, the officer in charge of the cadet Orthodox group. Dan became the cadet leader of the Orthodox group and some of his fondest West Point memories are tied to it: taking boat rides on the Hudson River, visiting the Greek Orthodox Cathedral in New York City and a Greek orphanage near West Point and developing lifelong bonds with fellow cadets like Kelly Campbell, who remains one of Dan's closest friends.

"From the day we checked in at the academy to the present day," Dan said, "Kelly and I have remained close friends as West Point brothers."

"I can do all things though Christ" has always been a guiding force for Dan. It is either fitting or prescient that he underlined that Philippians 4:13 passage in his West Point-issued Bible a couple of days before his accident. It is every bit as much a rallying point for Dan as "All the way and then some," one of the Army Ranger mottos that has resonated with him.

"Not that Dan didn't have rough moments, but he always came back to his faith," Bill said. "He's always had one phrase: 'When I get to Heaven, I'm going to have a new body.' That keeps him going."

Dan's faith lifted him five years after his accident when he reached an emotional crossroads. He had made tremendous progress in physical, speech, and occupational therapy. But Dan also recognized that he might never fully recover no matter how hard he worked. One morning, Dan struggled with this reality as he sat on the couch in the family game room. He was tired and frustrated. That moment may have been the closest Dan came to questioning the larger plan for him.

Then he heard a loud bang. He looked out the window and saw nothing. It got eerily quiet and a sense of peace washed over him.

"I felt the Holy Spirit within me," Dan said.

He went to the desk in the game room and found his small pocket Bible. Dan closed his eyes, opened his Bible, and pointed. When he opened his eyes, his finger was on Psalm 37:4. It reads: "Delight yourself in the Lord and He will give you the desires of your heart." The verse confirmed to Dan that he had just received a sign.

"From that moment on, my frustration has completely left me," Dan said, "and I accept the condition I am in and am thankful for what I have."

That seminal moment only strengthened Dan. It also made him a powerful example to people like Bob Weaver.

Weaver taught art and coached wrestling for almost two decades at Yough High School in western Pennsylvania. He became friends with Bill after Bill retired from Robert Morris University and became athletic director at Yough. After learning about Dan, Weaver invited him to speak to the school's Fellowship of Christian Athletes chapter.

"The students responded to him very well because he was very authentic," Weaver said. "A good example is more important than good advice. The fact that he had gone through all of that and had such a great perspective on life was just amazing. He's very unselfish even with all that he's gone through and all the difficulty that he's had. He has a heart for other people."

Dan's heart grabbed a couple of football coaches when he spoke at a Fellowship of Christian Athletes dinner in Pittsburgh. Bobby Bowden and Sam Rutigliano were the keynote speakers for the event at which Dan delivered the invocation. Bowden, then Florida State's head coach, was so impressed with Dan that he told the crowd, "I think you just heard the keynote speaker."

Rutigliano, the head coach of the Cleveland Browns from 1978-84, invited Dan to speak to his players at Liberty, a private Evangelical Christian university in Virginia. The time he spent with Dan made a lasting impression on Rutigliano.

"I will never, as long as I live, forget the inspiring talk that you gave to my players at Liberty University," Rutigliano wrote in a letter. "Dan, we saw Jesus in you that day, and don't forget how much you have done for His Kingdom. You have such a powerful testimony. You truly are a disciple. God bless you, Dan, and your wonderful mom and dad."

Long after he had retired from coaching, Rutigliano still marveled at Dan's faith and determination.

"With all of the places that I've been, all of the players that I've had, very few did what he has done," Rutigliano said. "I had players who got injuries and they didn't want to fight it. This guy had the rest of his life (to fight) but he didn't give up. A lot of my kids said, 'Gosh, Coach, I couldn't believe the impact that he had on our team.' Danny is a living, breathing epitome of what it means to stand your ground and refuse to give up. He made me feel good when I was trying to make him feel good."

Dan had the same effect on Joe Ravasio, the Ringgold football coach who had Dan speak to his team in 1987. More than thirty years later, Ravasio became emotional when he talked about Dan.

"As human beings we often wonder, 'Boy, what was the reason behind this tragedy or this accident?' " Ravasio said. "Then you see the great impact that Danny has had on others because he has never blamed the good Lord or said, 'Why me?' It's always been about 'How can I use my life to bless somebody else?' I think of that quite often, and it's had a great impact on me personally."

Ravasio paused and choked back sobs. With his voice barely above a whisper, he said, "I can honestly say that I wake up every day and I say to myself, 'What can I do today to bless another human being?' I take it very seriously, whether it's writing a card or a letter or making a phone call."

The question that always lingered after Dan's accident is what could have been.

The same question could have been asked about Bill, though on a much lesser scale.

He played in the NFL, yet never caught the break he needed to enjoy a long career. He left a good job as a salesman at Wrigley's so he could go back to school and eventually teach and coach football.

His coaching career never gained traction because life always seemed to get in the way. However, Bill did make an indelible impression on his players during his coaching years.

At California State College (now California University of Pennsylvania), Bill served as the defensive coordinator. He spent nights watching film on the living room wall at home, sometimes not shutting off the projector until four o'clock in the morning.

His players appreciated that Bill had played that game at the highest level and the nuances he taught them. Bill, a teacher in every sense of the word, coached without bombast or foul language.

"Never heard him curse," recalled former California State defensive back Tim Tracy. "He might say 'Gosh dang it.'"

Dave Villiotti remembers that expression as the extent of Bill's salty language when Bill was the head coach at Swissvale High School.

Like Tracy, Villiotti established a lifelong bond with Bill despite playing only one season for him.

That bond is so enduring it caused Villiotti to do some unexpected editing after he wrote, *We're From the Town with the Great Football*

Team: A Pittsburgh Steelers Manifesto. Villiotti sent his old coach a copy of the book online, but not before he did some scrubbing.

"I went back and deleted every swear word so I could send him a copy without that language in it," Villiotti said. "My brother said, 'Gee, how come you did that for Coach Priatko but not for our own mother?' That was the respect that I had for Bill Priatko. A humble guy and a superior human being."

Villiotti, now in his mid-sixties, added, "I talk to him and it's still like I'm a sixteen-year-old and he's my coach."

A coach who commanded respect from his players. A coach who had played the game at the highest level and understood the fundamentals and nuances of it. A coach who could teach the game to his players. Bill had all of those. Almost thirty years after they were together at California State, Tracy wrote Bill a letter and told him, "Coach, you are the best coach I ever had."

He still feels that way – and then some.

"There's no doubt in my mind that he would have been NFL level," Tracy said. "He was that good."

Bill ultimately chose his family over coaching, and everything else. He never regretted it, either.

His faith helped sustain him through those years when he worked several jobs for minimal pay and had little time to sleep. His prayers were literally answered when a Paul Brown recommendation landed him a job in Robert Morris' athletic department as an academic advisor and compliance officer.

Bill helped repay the school for hiring him with the impact he had on Robert Morris' student-athletes.

"He was somebody the athletes really respected," said Dr. Nell Hartley, who taught in Robert Morris' School of Business. "He told them they needed to do their homework or they were benched. They responded. Athletes do not forget him."

Mary "Mimi" Sams certainly didn't. Sams, whose maiden name is Reiber, spent a lot of time in Bill's office, though not because of academic issues. Sams, a point guard for the women's basketball team, sustained major knee injuries her junior and senior seasons. She struggled when the game was taken away from her. Nobody helped her more through the misery of being unable to play than Bill.

He always had a smile for her, words of encouragement, and a sympathetic ear. Bill also helped Sams deal with her father's illness. He died after a long battle with emphysema, shortly after Sams graduated. Bill was at the funeral. He was also at Sams's wedding years later, and the two have stayed in touch. When Bill met Sams's children a couple of years ago, they asked if they could adopt Bill as their grandfather. Is it any wonder why Sams calls "Mr. P" every Father's Day?

"That feeling that somebody cares so much about you as a person, especially as a young person, he made a lot of my days better," she said. "He was there to support me, someone whose shoulder I could cry on, laugh with me at my wedding. He means the world to me. I'm very, very blessed that he impacted my life."

Perhaps the best indicator of Bill's impact at Robert Morris came after he retired in 2005.

"He would come back for Homecoming and kids who had gone to the school years ago would still greet him the same way and introduce him to their husbands and wives and kids," said Don Smith, the school's Associate Athlete Director for Event Management and Facilities. "They just adored him. I think he genuinely cared for them and they could tell that."

His care extended beyond the athletes.

Hartley recalled how welcoming and respectful Bill was when she became the first female professor in Robert Morris' business school. She appreciated his work with her students as much as his decorum. That is why she stopped at school president Charles Sewall's office one day. Hartley had heard rumblings that Bill's job might be in jeopardy.

She never asked Bill about it, but she defended him by going to the top of the school's hierarchy.

"Now realize I'm a relatively new faculty member, just a couple of years under my belt, and I put my gradebook down on (Sewall's) desk and I went through the roster and said, 'Excuse me, President Sewall, but you need to know that the only reason that this, this and this student has been able to remain in school and play on your basketball team is because of Bill Priatko,'" she said. "I felt so strongly about Bill's effectiveness. That's how passionately I feel about him."

Years later, Hartley recommended Bill for the Robert Morris University Athletic Hall of Fame. She was among the first people he thanked during his 2015 induction speech.

What endeared Bill most to colleagues and students at Robert Morris was that he always was the same person and always made them feel like they were the most important person in his life.

"He would make you feel good," said Nick Cutich, who worked at Robert Morris in custodial services. "Talk to him and you would feel better already. He's always so positive."

He was so positive that people who didn't know Bill never would have guessed what he was dealing with at home, from Dan's recovery to Helen's cancer and later the stress of David twice serving in combat in the Middle East.

"You would have never known what he was going through," said Sams, who is a teacher and coach in the Orlando, Florida, area. "It almost feels like, 'Wow, I'm such a bad person (because) I didn't take that interest in him.' In your twenties you're still growing, you're still learning. I truly try to inspire my students to be like that, take an interest in other people; don't just worry about what you're going through."

Bill never took his problems to work or anywhere else, because, to him, everyone had something they were dealing with in their personal lives.

"They say God only gives you what you can handle. Well, Bill's handled a lot and you would never know it," said Dr. Philip Dahar, the orthodontist who is close with the Priatko family. "He inspires people and doesn't need to be inspired. He'd give you the shirt off his back. Very, very Christian-minded. He accepts what happens and that's the way Bill is."

The Priatkos could have been set for life financially after Dan's accident. The wreck occurred on a stretch of Route 81 that did not have a guardrail. The Priatkos had grounds for a lawsuit against the Pennsylvania Department of Transportation for negligence, especially since there were more than twenty car accidents on Route 81 in the Hazleton area that day.

They never seriously considered suing, even though Bill said they could have made "millions of dollars." They even declined to extend the statute of limitations on litigation in case they changed their mind.

Dan's medical bills were paid through various insurance policies, and, to the Priatkos, a lawsuit would have kept them looking back on the accident instead of moving forward from it. Eschewing litigation was symbolic of the approach the family took after Dan's accident.

"It happened. You can't change it," Bill said. "Accept it. We have."

Bill struggled with guilt in the aftermath of the car accident. As he stood beside Dan's bed in the Intensive Care Unit at Hazleton Hospital, he wondered if it was somehow his fault that Dan was fighting for his life. Had he done something to anger God?

There was nothing rational about such thinking. Bill had always sacrificed for his family. He did not appear to have a malicious bone in his body. But as a grief-stricken parent, he was trying to make sense out of something that made no sense. That immense strain and sadness caused his mind to unspool as Bill searched for any clue as to what he could have done differently.

The haunting thoughts did not push Bill away from religion; they propelled him toward it. One reason why Bill's faith never wavered is because of what he and his family experienced prior to Dan's accident. Some of it simply couldn't be explained beyond a higher power.

Kathy, Bill and Helen's youngest child, had been marked for death at nine months old after she was rushed to the hospital with a severe bronchial infection. Roughly ten hours elapsed between Dr. Martin Murcek telling Bill there was nothing more that could be done for Kathy to Kathy breathing on her own again. Nothing medically could be attributed to Kathy's miraculous recovery.

During that time, Helen had a vision while sleeping, and interpreted it as a sign from God that Kathy would rise. At the hospital, as Father Igor Soroka prayed with Bill, he set an icon of the Virgin Mary next to Kathy's face. He and Bill left the room for a few minutes. When they returned the icon was on the other side of Kathy's face.

Soroka asked the only nurse in the ICU if she had moved the icon. She hadn't touched it. Kathy couldn't have moved since she was hooked up to a respirator, her tiny body tethered by tubes.

Nine hours later she was breathing on her own.

Soroka returned to the hospital after Kathy was out of danger. She was in a small oxygen tent to help with her breathing. Soroka, with Kathy facing away from him, held up a small cross outside of the tent.

"Kathy," he said, "kiss the cross."

Kathy rolled over and crawled to the cross. She lifted her head up and kissed it as Soroka, Bill, and Helen watched in amazement. She had never crawled or talked, so there was no earthly way to explain what had just happened.

Almost forty years later, Bill said, "I can remember the scene like it was yesterday, and it was like you couldn't believe what you were watching."

Something similar happened in 2007 when the Priatko children treated Bill and Helen to a trip to Moscow for their fiftieth wedding anniversary. Dan and Debbie went with them.

One day, they were touring the Red Square when the skies suddenly turned angry. Bill told Helen and Debbie to run to the tour bus, which was about 400 yards away beneath an underpass. He started pushing Dan's wheelchair as fast as he could. He went even faster after a bolt of lightning hit nearby pavement and caused sparks.

Suddenly, two muscular men appeared. It was if they had materialized out of the mist. Each picked up a side of Dan's wheelchair and took off toward the bus. They ran so fast that Bill had trouble keeping up with them.

Bill caught up with them at the bus and thanked them in Russian. He started to pull out his wallet to give them money, but they refused it, saying "Nyet (No) Nyet (No)!"

They were gone as quickly as they had appeared.

After everyone was safely back on the bus, Bill tried to make sense of something so surreal. He told a woman sitting near him the story. The woman, a professor at the University of Connecticut, told him they were guardian angels who had been sent to take care of his son.

"You know what ma'am?" Bill said. "I think you're right."

Bill is certain he and Dan would have been struck by lightning if not for those two men. He is just as certain that they were saved by guardian angels.

"There's no way two men could appear like they did and disappear like they did," Bill said.

Guardian angels have come in many forms to the Priatkos throughout the years. One was Rev. Bernard Murphy and his wife, Jane. The Murphys insisted that Bill and Helen stay with them in Hazleton and prayed with them every morning and every night. Their church prayed for Dan every Sunday. That support lifted them when they needed it most. That is why it meant so much to Bill and Helen when Dan returned to Hazleton a couple of years after the accident.

Dan spoke one Sunday at the Methodist church where countless prayers had been said for him. His mere presence at the church left people he had never met in tears. Ruth Hughes, a nurse at Hazleton Hospital who had cared for Dan, was the church organist that Sunday. Dan's neurologist at Hazleton Hospital was also in attendance.

That morning, Christian Orthodox congregants and a Jewish neurologist prayed with Methodists and rejoiced over Dan's recovery. To Murphy, the poignant scene could be distilled to one thing: people coming together over the shared belief that there is indeed a higher power.

"Without God," Murphy said, "we're lost."

God has always seemed to put people the Priatkos' lives at exactly the right time. It happened in 2010 when Dan came down with a rash on his left arm. It seemed relatively harmless at first, but it soon landed Dan in Presbyterian Hospital. His arm ballooned from his wrist to his shoulder and dermatologists were at a loss to explain the massive swelling.

"If you looked at his arm it was hideous," Bill said. "It was tough to see."

The situation became dire. Doctors told Bill and Helen that they might have to amputate Dan's arm to stem the infection.

Bill and Helen were crushed, and they knew Dan would be devastated if he lost his arm. The right side of his body had already been compromised by the car accident. Losing his left arm would confine him to a wheelchair for the rest of his life.

They stayed positive and did not share with Dan what doctors had told them. His condition slowly improved but Dan still had a lot of work ahead of him to make his arm functional. They met with a rehabilitation doctor and learned they had a connection with her.

Dr. Tiffany Starks was the wife of Steelers offensive tackle Max Starks. She was just as affable as her husband, a two-time Super Bowl winner with the Steelers. Her compassion and encouragement made her the perfect doctor for Dan. Rehabilitation worked, saving Bill and Helen a conversation they had dreaded.

"What the heck would have happened if he would have had to revert to a wheelchair completely?" Bill said. "I don't even want to think about what the outcome could be. Thank heavens that wasn't the case."

Greg Petrick lives outside of Washington, D.C. but sometimes drives through Pennsylvania when he visits his son in New Hampshire. When Petrick, who is retired from the Air Force and works as a contractor, opts for the scenic route over Route 95, it takes him past the site of Dan's car accident. That may be his most visceral reminder of what Dan lost in the accident. It is not the only one.

When Petrick thinks of Dan, he calls to mind General George C. Marshall's famous quote, stating that if he needed someone to carry out a really dangerous mission in World War II, he wanted a West Point football player.

"If it was hard, Dan would volunteer to do it," Petrick said.

Everything in his life attests to that. He has never shied away from a challenge, and prior to his accident, Dan appeared to be on an ascendant path in the army. He was driven, disciplined, and smart, and he had distinguished himself at West Point and beyond by graduating from Army Ranger School.

He was wired to succeed, and anybody who knows Dan is convinced he could have gone as far as he had wanted to in the Army. Maybe even become a general.

"People would naturally gravitate to his leadership style," said Dr. Andrew Glen, Dan's West Point classmate. "Young. Smart. Handsome.

A West Point football player. He really had everything going for him. Now does that turn into him making general or colonel? Who knows? But Dan would have been an exceptional leader wherever he would have been assigned."

To put into perspective of how high Dan might have climbed, West Point superintendent Daryl A. Williams is a lieutenant general who previously served as commander of the NATO Allied Land Command. Williams graduated a year ahead of Dan, and they were football teammates.

Dan celebrated his fifty-eighth birthday on March 19, 2020. If not for the accident, he may have been in a top position like Williams.

"Can you imagine, if Dan wouldn't have gotten hurt, what he would have been today?" said Bob Ford, a close family friend who knew Dan before the accident. "I don't see why he couldn't have been a general with the leadership skills that he has and how much he was respected. Everything he's done, he's risen to the top with leadership."

That includes what happened after his accident. The tragedy didn't rob Dan of leadership; it simply conferred a different kind of leadership on him.

"If there wasn't a Dan that was able to do the things that he's done and help people, their lives could have changed in a negative way where they would lose hope and give up, and in some cases there are people who blame God, and that's a terrible thing when that happens," Father Igor Soroka said. "Dan was able to intervene in the lives of so many people by what he went through and give them new hope. He's not finished yet. He may be only at the beginning of what he's going to do. We just don't know."

What is known is that Dan has touched countless people simply by being Dan.

"Everybody has a purpose in life, and it would be easy to say his purpose was to graduate from West Point and be an officer and get married and have children," said Kathy Sekera, Dan's younger sister.

"Well, his purpose is to spread the message and gospel of Jesus Christ and to be an inspiration to many, because it's obvious with his life that he's done that. He's impacted many more people on a daily basis than he probably would have prior to that." He's impacted many more people on a daily basis than he probably would have prior to that."

Sometimes Dan surprises even those closest to him with his testimony.

Dan once spoke to a group of Norwin High School seniors at St. Stephen's Byzantine Catholic Church in North Huntingdon. After his talk, a girl asked Dan if it bothered him to know what he could have been. He said, "If anything that I said to you here just brings one of you, one of you, closer to Jesus Christ, then I'm glad my accident happened."

As they were driving home, Bill said, "Dan, I never heard you say that."

Dan smiled and shrugged. There was really nothing more to say.

Barbara Tray taught Dan at Norwin High School. She never forgot what she called Dan's "quiet smile" or the time he sent her a thank you letter from West Point for pushing him in English class. Like many who knew Dan, Tray shed her share of tears after his accident.

Five years after Dan's accident, she cried because of who Dan still is.

Following the birth of her only child in 1990, Tray received a congratulatory card in the mail. When she opened it, the card was signed by Dan. He had also enclosed a $25 check. Tray had not seen Dan in a couple of years and had no idea that he knew about her daughter, Kylie. The enormity of the gesture overwhelmed her. She cried for twenty minutes.

"I still get choked up and still get goosebumps every time I think about it," Tray said nearly three decades later. "You talk about special. Danny's always had a place in my heart, and he always will."

Such feelings sometimes made her question why such a cruel fate had befallen Dan. What always gave her hope was the response of Dan and his family to Dan's accident and to the cancer that Dan's mother battled for years.

"I just find it absolutely amazing that they have remained the people that they are," Tray said. "They are an amazing family and truly an inspiration. Sometimes we don't get the whole picture. There has to be a reason out there. We just don't know what it is."

The question of *Why Dan?* is one that Dan Wukich pondered, especially after he and Dan grew close when Dan worked for him at Loyalhanna Care Center.

"He's one of the best human beings I have ever met," Wukich said. "It's one of those things where you back off and say, 'What is God doing? Are you sure you've got the right guy?' "

If that question has ever been posed by Dan, nobody has heard it. Nor has Dan ever complained about the challenges the accident left him to face. A lingering one involves sleep. The part of Dan's brain that controls sleep was irreparably damaged in the accident. He has since dealt with chronic sleep deprivation and often can't fall asleep until three or four o'clock in the morning. When Bill calls him "Father Dan," it's not just because Dan knows the Bible so well. It is also because he often reads his Bible deep into the night due to his sleeping struggles.

Despite the fatigue that is a daily reality for Dan, he never uses it as an excuse to skip work or a workout at the local Planet Fitness. Or to simply allow himself to be in a bad mood. In that sense Dan has never changed from what Frank Klanchar remembers from their football days together at Norwin High School.

"Dan would never be a complainer," said Klanchar, who was a team captain his senior season along with Dan and Ernie Furno. "Even after a tough practice or if we had a really bad game, he kind of just put those things behind him right away. Almost like a hockey goalie: if you give up a goal you just have to forget about it and you move forward."

Moving forward is something Dan has always done. That approach elicits admiration but not surprise for those who know him well.

"Maybe he's had dark periods. Maybe he still has them," said Kevin Donnelly, Dan's classmate and football teammate at Norwin. "But you'll never know. I'll never know because he will not put that burden on someone else of 'Hey, I'm having a bad day today.' It's always 'Hey, I'm going to the gym today' or 'I just came back from a luncheon' or 'I just spoke with so and so.' He never complains."

Donnelly spent more than thirty years in law enforcement in Miami-Dade County in South Florida. He worked as an undercover narcotics detective and teamed with DEA and FBI agents on various task forces. He has seen a lot of bad things and has a pretty good read on when the perception of someone changes because something life-altering has happened to them—and whether such change is genuine.

"Someone could have been a piece of garbage and all of the sudden something tragic happens to them and now they're this great person," said Donnelly, who is retired. "That's not Dan's case. He was always a good person, maintained his personality, his drive. For a lot of us, we thought he had life by the short hairs. Something really turned him upside down but that didn't change him. That's very impressive to me. You look back and knew this guy was going to be important."

To Donnelly, the accident only changed how Dan was going to make a difference.

"He didn't lose his desire to be, but something made him move in a different direction," Donnelly said. "He took it and just ran with it. He's an inspiration to a lot of people."

He is to Bob Flaherty. The former Norwin football teammates stay in touch through email, and Dan's approach to life has helped Flaherty.

"He finds the positive in everything," said Flaherty, who lives in Carmel, Indiana. "He's got such a deep faith in God, and this is what God has planned for him, to make a difference in other people's lives.

He's doing what he can for other people and sees that as his gift to everybody, and it is an absolute gift."

Dan with Bob Flaherty in the game room of the Priatko house

That gift sometimes manifests itself in the mundane.

"When I see his emails and (read) them, I'll just smile and start laughing, sometimes at work," Flaherty said. "It makes me feel good and he's got a way of doing that. I hope I can provide him half of what he gives to me or even a quarter of what he gives to me. I love him like a brother, I really do. I'm blessed to know him."

Dan has always supplied perspective to those close with him. Sometimes he does it with a twist of humor.

One time, Kathy was driving and becoming increasingly agitated with the plodding driver in front of her. Dan, who was in the passenger seat, told her to let it go. The driver in front of them was practicing for

Sunday, he told her in reference to the day of the week once reserved for leisurely drives. Kathy laughed, and her stress evaporated.

Dan has a terrific sense of humor, as Irwin barber Don Nagy learned one day after cutting Dan and Bill's hair. Bill had been joking with his good friend that he was the best barber around. The two engaged in some good-natured ribbing, but Dan got the last word. As he and Bill were leaving Don's Barber Salon, Dan said, "Don, you're a cut above."

Dan can deliver such lines with impeccable timing.

Bob "Bo" Garritano discovered this gift of Dan's when they were in the same seating section for a Norwin football game. Garritano had brought a small stadium seat with nylon netting on the sides of it. During the game, he leaned too far forward for the netting to keep him in the seat and toppled over. Had someone been sitting right below Garritano, he would have landed on top of them. Garritano was mortified as he got up, certain that everybody in the stadium was looking at him.

Dan didn't miss a beat.

"I think you need a seatbelt for that seat," he said to the chastened Garritano.

What else could Garritano do? He laughed out loud.

"It was," he said, "the funniest thing ever."

Dick LeBeau achieved football immortality in 2010 when he was inducted into the Pro Football Hall of Fame.

The one person LeBeau wanted to share the honor with most wasn't there to see it. His mother, Beulah, had passed away, but the younger of her two sons made sure she was part of his special night. She had always been his biggest supporter and said for years that he deserved to be in the Hall of Fame. During his induction speech, LeBeau subtly pointed to the sky and said softly, "Well, Beulah, we're here."

There is a reason why LeBeau called his mother every night, why he broke away from the Steelers' Super Bowl party in 2009 after they had won their sixth Lombardi Trophy just so he could make a phone call: Beulah LeBeau meant everything to him.

She raised LeBeau and his older brother, Bob, by herself. They never wanted for anything because of her resolve. One Easter, she needed material so she could make baskets for her sons. She walked three miles round trip just so her sons could have authentic Easter baskets.

"Who does that? Only mothers," LeBeau said. "In most American homes, the glue is the mother."

LeBeau saw that in Dan's mother, Helen, after he got to know her when he started coaching for the Steelers. LeBeau couldn't help but notice how Helen took care of Dan and her family, even as she battled cancer.

"Helen always reminded me of my mother," he said paying her the ultimate compliment. "They were cut from the same cloth. Both were reasonably small in stature but tremendously strong in spirit and will."

Nothing showed that more than the fight Helen took to cancer.

She never let it slow her down or dampen her preternatural kindness. Her outpatient treatment consisted of getting the cancerous cells scraped off her bladder and then enduring chemotherapy. Upon returning home, Helen never headed straight to bed as many would have. Instead, she started making dinner or doing laundry or some other household chore.

Her indomitable will inspired everyone around her, especially Dan. And Dan kept Helen going because she wanted to make sure he would always be taken care of.

Bill and Helen in a 50th wedding anniversary photo in 2007

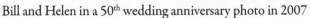

Helen's care for people extended beyond Dan and her own family. For years, next-door neighbor Shirley Yohman cared for her mother and her mother-in-law, both of whom were paralyzed. Helen helped Shirley keep the house clean. She also stayed with her mother and mother-in-law when Shirley needed someone while she was out. Helen fed them and cared for them as if they were her own family. That's just who she was.

And Shirley never heard Helen complain about anything.

"She was just a very, very lovely woman," Shirley said.

After staring down cancer for almost thirty years, Helen was diagnosed with a different form of bladder of cancer in 2014. Her urologist, Dr. James McCague, told her she probably had five more years to live. But the cancer spread with such ferocity there was nothing the doctors could do.

The cancer ravaged her pelvic region, leaving her unable to walk and without an appetite.

One day Helen fell off the couch in the family game room. There is no carpeting in that room and Helen was too weak from the cancer to get up. Dan was home alone with her and he knew the right person to call.

Henry Yohman, Shirley's husband, had always been *that* neighbor who could help with anything. Bill couldn't count the number of times he couldn't get a stubborn lawnmower to start. Henry would come over and fix the problem. One year, all of the Christmas lights went out at the Priatko house. Bill called Henry, and he knew what to do.

His biggest assist came when he gingerly scooped up Helen off the floor and got her back on the couch. She was lucky she hadn't been seriously hurt and Helen told him, "Henry you're always so kind to me and you're always helping us."

That night Bill got a phone call from Henry, who asked him how Helen was doing. He was perplexed until Henry explained what had happened. Helen had not told Bill about it because she did not want to worry him. She never wanted to make it about her and was that way until the very end.

One day in June 2014, an ambulance was summoned to take Helen to Mercy Hospital in Pittsburgh. Helen was in such bad shape that her family knew she was probably leaving home for the final time. What did Helen do? She politely asked the ambulance driver not to turn on the flashing lights because she didn't want to alarm the neighbors.

She died on June 25 at the age of eighty-one. Bill and her four kids were with her when she passed.

Lines formed around the block for her viewings. The family accepted condolences for hours. Dorothy Tragesser, the speech therapist who had worked with Dan after his accident, knew how physically hard it was for Dan to stand for that long. But there was no chance he was sitting down, not after the fight he had seen his mother wage for years.

When Tragesser hugged Dan at one of the viewings, she said, "Dan, you kept your mother alive for so many years. She stayed alive for you. What a wonderful woman."

That sentiment was shared by John Varoscak, who had grown up a couple of row houses down from Helen in Braddock. During that time, Bill had looked after him as if he was a little brother. Bill took him to sporting events, keeping him away from the kind of trouble that was easy to find. Varoscak became a standout basketball player, eventually earning a full athletic scholarship to Louisville.

To Varoscak, Bill and Helen were the perfect complement to one another. And the perfect couple to weather all the adversity that the family faced.

"Never bitter," Varoscak said of Helen. "Not, 'Oh Lord, why me?' Bill never said, 'Why me?' None of that."

The couple's makeup helps explain some things about them that are almost impossible to explain from a medical standpoint.

Helen defied the odds for years by beating back cancer. Bill, meanwhile, is an ageless marvel.

Now eighty-eight, he still does 155 push-ups every weekday in just two sets. Bill adds two extra push-ups on Mondays so he can get to 777 pushups for the week. (The number is significant to Bill since seven is his favorite number and Jesus Christ made seven final statements while on the cross). Bill also walks three miles a day.

"They were those wonderfully reliable, down-to-earth, faithful people, and I think that kind of thing spills over to your physiology," said McCague, Helen's longtime urologist. "I think that kind of gives you a good integration with the world but also with your health and your ability to deal with things. I'd probably find that really hard to prove in a science paper, but they were very, very special people."

Bill continues to stay young by working twenty-five hours a week during summers at Kennywood Park outside of Pittsburgh.

He has been working at one of the amusement park's drink stands for almost twenty consecutive summers, and it has turned into his hobby. Bill loves being around people and seeing "kids" he taught or worked with while at working in education.

To some, Bill is as synonymous with Kennywood as its roller coasters and Potato Patch fries. His association with Kennywood goes back eighty years, from when he first started going to the park. He started working there while still in high school.

"I had the pleasure to have as my boss the late Bob Henninger," Bill said. "Now, his grandson, Mike Henninger, is my boss. The park's general manager, Jerome Gibas is so kind to me along with staff members Joe Barron and Mike Paradise. I appreciate so much what they are doing for me."

Gibas showed his appreciation in ways that touched Bill deeply. One time in a newspaper article, Gibas said, "My two favorite Steelers were Jack Butler and Bill Priatko."

He expressed a similar sentiment at the opening of Kennywood's Steel Curtain rollercoaster in 2019. A handful of current Steelers and alumni attended it, including perennial Pro Bowl defensive end Cameron Heyward and offensive lineman Matt Feiler.

"You guys are outstanding Steelers," Gibas said during the presentation, "but Bill's my favorite."

Bill had considered riding the new rollercoaster. He knew he made the right decision to take a pass after former Steelers guard Craig Wolfley got off the Steel Curtain and was a little wobbly. The colorful Wolfley, a sideline reporter for Steelers' broadcasts, delivered the perfect line about the Steel Curtain while he and his family were eating lunch with Bill and iconic Pittsburgh broadcaster Bill Hillgrove: "I was more scared riding this thing than facing Joe Greene in the Oklahoma Drill at training camp."

Bill and Helen with Franco and Dana Harris at a 40th anniversary celebration of Harris's "Immaculate Reception." Franco and Dana are among Bill's good friends.

Staying busy has helped Bill cope with the loss of Helen.

Not long after losing Helen, Bill wrote to LeBeau. He thanked LeBeau for his friendship to him and Helen and told him how highly Helen thought of him.

LeBeau sent a letter from Steelers training camp. The final line still resonates with Bill.

"Helen was a great lady, and we will all miss her so much," LeBeau wrote on Steelers stationary. "I am very grateful that she approved of me. I take some comfort knowing that she is with Our Lord, and we will all be together again."

Chapter VII

BOOK OF DAN

B ill Priatko learned many lessons from his mother, especially about weathering adversity. Catherine Priatko did just that after she was widowed at the age of twenty-nine with five children. The kids ranged in age from three to thirteen, yet Catherine never flinched. She cleaned houses and worked in school cafeterias and nursing homes while still playing a central role in her children's lives.

Her work ethic and resolve left an indelible imprint on the youngest of her three sons. So did the time he was sitting at the dining room table and his mother held up the Bible she was reading.

"Billy," she said, "remember this is the truth and nothing else matters."

Bill never forgot that, and his mother's Bible is one of his most cherished possessions. It is the Bible that he and Helen prayed with right after receiving the life-changing phone call from Debbie. It is the Bible that Bill and Helen were praying with when they received a badly needed sign from God a couple of weeks after the accident.

It is also the Bible that Bill read in the Intensive Care Unit at Hazleton Hospital after arriving there with Helen.

Bill instinctively went to the Book of Daniel. He had read it to Dan when Dan was a young boy. He turned to it as Dan was fighting for his life.

Chapter 10 provided solace to Bill as he sat in the ICU waiting room. It was about a messenger God had sent to a weakened Daniel to give him strength, and about Daniel rising.

Bill saw parallels between Daniel and Dan. He started a tradition that continues to this day: every night Bill reads Chapter 10 in the Book of Daniel.

Dan has authored his own remarkable story after his life took a tragic turn. His perseverance, positivity, and faith inspired just about everybody who got to know him. Or who simply saw his example.

No book about Dan would be complete without West Point and Norwin and their meaning to Dan and his meaning to them. Or about the role Dan's faith played in shaping him before, and especially after, his accident.

And any book on Dan would have to start with—and now end with—his family and how central they are to his story.

Recognizing that I volunteered as a Ranger, fully knowing the hazards of my chosen profession, I will always endeavor to uphold the prestige, honor, and high esprit de corps of the Rangers. Acknowledging the fact that a Ranger is a more elite soldier who arrives at the cutting edge of battle by land, sea, or air, I accept the fact that as a Ranger my country expects me to move further, faster, and fight harder than any other soldier.

Never shall I fail my comrades. I will always keep myself mentally alert, physically strong, and morally straight, and I will shoulder more than my share of the task whatever it may be and then some.

*Gallantly will I show the world that I am a specially
selected and well-trained soldier. My courtesy to superior
officers, neatness of dress, and care of equipment shall set
the example for others to follow.*

*Energetically will I meet the enemies of my country. I
shall defeat them on the field of battle for I am better
trained and will fight with all my might. Surrender is
not a Ranger word. I will never leave a fallen comrade
to fall into the hands of the enemy, and under no circumstances will I ever embarrass my country.*

*Readily will I display the intestinal fortitude required to
fight on to the Ranger objective and complete the mission
though I be the lone survivor.*

Rangers Lead The Way!

The last stanza of the Army Ranger Creed always makes David
Priatko think of Dan.

"Every day he gets up and just kind of fights on to the next objective,"
David said of his older brother. "He always inspired me, and I always
wanted to be like him and do what he did. Then he had his accident
and the roles were kind of reversed."

Dan was still in a coma when David left for West Point in July
1985. He was determined to finish something that Dan was not able
to because of his catastrophic injuries. David took that as seriously as
his West Point oath, and it is reflected in his service.

He fought in Operation Desert Storm and in Operation Iraqi
Freedom. David won four Bronze Stars, which are awarded for war-
time valor and heroism. He retired from the Army in 2012 as a lieutenant colonel, after twenty-four years of service.

David, in West Point and U.S. Army portrait pictures, made Dan and his family proud.

One thing that has never changed through the years: Dan's hero status to his brother.

"In life, especially in the military and deployments, you go through tough times, and I always reminded myself what Dan had to go through when they said he wouldn't live, and if he did, he'd be two percent functional," David said. "Dan never complained. He persevered. He was strong in his faith, and he inspired so many people, especially me."

While David was in the army, he completed something of a circle for him, Dan, and Bill.

Dan and David had become enthralled with the military at a young age because of Bill's experiences. Bill's strong sense of duty had been sharpened as a young man by Frankie Korbel and Paul Olson. Bill never forgot that both made the ultimate sacrifice. The flag that Bill flies outside of the Priatko home every Memorial Day is the one the Olson family gave him from Paul's casket after he was killed in South Korea.

David knew how much Olson meant to his father. For the 50th anniversary of the outbreak of the Korean War, he took Bill and Helen to the spot where Olson had been killed by North Korean troops. It took David, who was stationed in South Korea at the time, about a month to pinpoint the location after he had worked on it with South Korean military liaisons and local government officials.

While his parents visited David, they went to a hillside near the Nakdong River. Olson and his regiment had made a valiant stand there but were vastly outnumbered by North Korean troops. When Bill thanked a local commissioner for his help providing him with some closure, the commissioner told him, "Thank your friend who gave us freedom."

Bill packed dirt from the area into a small container and returned home with it. He and his two brothers, both of whom had fought in World War II, conducted a short service for Olson at the cemetery and buried the dirt in his grave.

David, who lives in Toccoa, Georgia, and runs an ROTC program at a nearby high school, has all of Olson's service patches. They were given to him by Olson's family, and he has preserved them, so they stay in mint condition.

He has another prominent reminder of where he came from at his northeastern Georgia house.

A couple of years after his mother died, David had a street sign made for his driveway. Fittingly, he named it St. Helen, surprising Bill, Dan, and Debbie with the sign when they visited him. He also took them to a nearby village named Helen. They walked around and reminisced about Helen, certain that she was with them.

David and Bill with a special street sign

Dan and David have always been together, especially in spirit. Nothing conveys that better than a one-page letter on weathered paper that Bill kept. It is dated February 22, 1991, when David was fighting in Operation Desert Storm. David sent it to Dan before his birthday because he didn't know where he would be over the next couple of weeks:

Dan,

I do not have any fancy poems or elaborate words to send, but I just wanted to express my feeling in brother to brother talk. You have always been an inspiration to me throughout my life. I saw what you were able to achieve and realized my goals were not impossible. I saw that you were senior class president and graduated from West Point. I knew, from your example, that I could also do those things if I put my mind and heart into it. Above all, I will never forget your faith and determination that has brought you a long way from the day that you were seriously injured in your accident. I know that struggles remain ahead, but you have what it takes to weather the storms in life. I am thankful that I have been given a brother who has positively inspired me to do good things. Many are not as fortunate as me. I wish you all of God's blessings and pray that God will grant you many happy and healthful years. I look forward to seeing you soon.

Love,
David

David had to deal with tragedy after he retired from the Army. In 2018, his wife, Dottie, died at the age of fifty-three of complications from cancer. In addition to David, she left behind a daughter, Michaela, and a son, David.

"We're doing okay," David said. "I know she lived a life of faith, and I know she's not suffering anymore. I tell people grief is kind of like the tide. Sometimes it comes in and hits you hard and other times it's not so bad."

David and the kids took a vacation to Europe a year after Dottie's death. She had always told him to live life to the fullest and to make time for things such as family vacations. It was his way of honoring his wife.

That fall, he took his son David shopping before his freshman year of college. He told his namesake the story of how his mother had taken him and his siblings shopping for school clothes when he was growing up; how she had resolutely walked them to a bus stop and then back after getting all of them new clothes.

It is a quintessential Priatko story, one that needed to be passed down.

ebbie was in the car with Dan when he lost control of it, and she is the only one who remembers anything about the accident. She can still recall how drastically the weather changed, how Dan became extra cautious while behind the wheel.

"The next thing I knew we were fishtailing," Debbie said. "I put my hand on the dashboard and went, 'Oh my God!'"

The next thing Debbie remembered was waking up in a haze as emergency responders cut open the car to get to her and Dan. She looked over at Dan and he was slumped over the steering wheel.

Then she passed out again. She called Bill from Hazleton Hospital and told him that Dan was fighting for his life. She also kept saying that he had to call Joseph and Helen Bergantz, with whom they had stayed that weekend. Dan and Debbie had promised them before leaving West Point that they would get home safely.

"We didn't make it, Dad," she told Bill.

Debbie's life didn't change as drastically as Dan's after the accident. But she stepped up as much as anyone when her family needed her. She spent countless hours after work at the hospital with Dan, and later Helen.

She took Dan walking and swimming as part of his physical therapy, often doing things nobody saw. That included giving Dan the blood thinning shots he needed and remaining a constant presence in his life, even at the expense of her own social life.

Debbie never grappled with survivor's guilt. That is not to say she didn't struggle as she watched Dan work so hard just to be able to walk and talk again.

"I cried a lot because I knew what he was and what he had become and I knew what he could have been," Debbie said.

Her voice cracked before she continued, "I will tell you now, that if that was me, I'm not sure I could do it. I'm not sure I could have handled it the way he did. He's an inspiration."

But Debbie is an inspiration to Dan and Bill. She lives with them and has assumed the caretaker role that Helen filled for so many years. Bill is many things; handy in the kitchen is not among them. One story that will get passed down in family lore is the time Bill remarked that the soup he had found in the refrigerator and reheated tasted funny. That's because it was gravy. (Irony: Bill once taught home economics for a couple of months at General Braddock High School, and at the end of the school year, students petitioned for him to stay in that role.)

Debbie keeps such kitchen mishaps to a minimum by cooking for Bill and Dan and taking care of the house after long days of work. Debbie is an executive assistant at University of Pittsburgh Medical Center (UPMC) and her days often start with a four o'clock wake-up call.

"I don't know what I'd do without her," Bill said. "I think Dan and I would be eating at Wendy's every night. She's got a tough job. Sometimes she doesn't get home until seven o'clock. Debbie's been a blessing."

Sometimes Debbie's responsibilities, including serving as secretary of St. Nicholas Orthodox Church, wear her down. But anytime she gets frustrated, Dan puts everything into perspective.

"At times I'll just gripe and my brother will say, 'What are you complaining about?' " Debbie said. "He would love to do all of that. I just shut up and I look at him and say, 'You are so right.' He looks at things differently, and sometimes that helps you because that makes you look at them differently."

He has also done that with Kathy Sekera, the youngest of the Priatko children.

"We might complain about our daily issues," Kathy said, "and then we look at Dan, and it's a struggle for him to brush his teeth or walk down the stairs, and it takes him three times as long to do something we do in a spilt second."

What may have meant as much to Kathy as much as it did to Dan was something the older of her two sons did to honor his uncle in 2019.

Every Penn-Trafford High School senior player was profiled in the football program with quick-hitting items that ranged from favorite quotes to future plans. For his biggest inspiration, Kurtis Sekera wrote, "Uncle Dan. Just having him there and what he's done. It helped me get back where I could play part of my senior season."

Kurtis tore his ACL his junior season and had to work through the pain and drudgery of rehabilitation to get back on the field. As hard as it was, he always reminded himself that others had to go through worse. He always thought of Dan.

When Dan saw what Kurtis had written in the program, he started shaking, his way of sobbing. Kurtis didn't tell anyone in his family that he was going to name Dan as his greatest inspiration. No one suggested he do it. It came from the heart.

If Kurtis exemplifies the familial love and support that binds Dan and his extended family, he likely gets it from his mother.

Just as Debbie assumed a primary caretaker role after Helen died, Kathy did the same after Debbie was diagnosed with breast cancer in 2017. Kathy went with her older sister to every doctor's appointment and radiation treatment. The cancer is in remission, and Debbie credits the fight she took to beat it to her family and her faith.

"I've seen my brother. I've seen my mom," Debbie said. "We've had so much adversity in our family that we know how to handle it. We also know God's in control, and no matter what we say or what we do, it's ultimately His decision."

A monument to Helen hangs in the game room of the Priatko home. It is a plaque that Bill and her children gave her for Mother's Day in 1991. A gold plate on the bottom half of the plaque unfurls a poem on which Bill and his children collaborated:

FROM THE DAY THAT SHE SAID, "I WILL
LOVE AND OBEY"
A WONDERFUL WOMAN SHE HAS BEEN
IN EVERY WAY
SHE EXEMPLIFIES ALWAYS THE BEST
IN A MOTHER
NEVER PUTTING HERSELF
BEFORE ANOTHER

WASHING & IRONING, TENDERLY CARING
FOR KATHY & DEBBIE
ALWAYS DOING HER BEST TO HAVE
THEM READY
FROM MORNING TILL NIGHT ON A
DEVOTED WHIRL
PROUDLY PRIMPING DANNY AND DAVID'S
'DIPPITY-DO' CURL
SHE TRULY IS A CHRISTIAN MOTHER
TEACHING HER CHILDREN TO LOVE
ONE ANOTHER
TO MY FAMILY AND I SHE IS
THE VERY BEST
SOMEDAY WITH OUR LORD SHE WILL
HAVE ETERNAL REST
TO MY PRECIOUS AND DEAR WIFE
WITH ALL MY LOVE ON MOTHER'S DAY
MAY 12, 1991

The top half of the plaque has six pictures – five of them are Helen and the kids in different stages of their lives; the other one is of the family with Father Igor Soroka in front St. Nicholas Orthodox Church.

Helen loved nothing more than being with her children and taking care of her family. Her children are a testament to the job she did as a mother.

"I have so much respect, praise, and honor for Mr. and Mrs. Priatko and what they have done for those four kids," said Al Lynn, who taught in the Norwin school district and coached Dan and David in football. "You talk about a model family. That's the Priatkos. All four (children) I'm sure have so much love in their hearts for their dad, for their mom, and I'm sure their mom is looking down on them, smiling, because all of them were great."

The extended Priatko family during Helen's last Christmas in 2013. From front: David Priatko, Kristopher Sekera, Michaela Priatko, and Kathy Sekera. From top: Kurtis Sekera, Debbie, Dottie Priatko, David, Dan, Bill, and Helen. The photo was taken by Kathy's husband, Keith.

Helen was gravely ill when Bill gave her a Mother's Day card in 2014. In the card, he wrote, "Our Lord knows what you mean to me. Thanks for being a wonderful mother to our children. May God grant you many years."

Helen couldn't walk, yet she insisted on getting Bill a card for Father's Day. Debbie picked one out for her, and Helen signed it "All my love Forever, Katrinka." Katrinka is the affectionate nickname Bill called Helen from when they were young (Helen's blonde pigtails reminded Bill of a little Dutch girl).

Helen wrote "Forever Katrinka" twice on the card, both times in squiggly cursive strokes. That betrayed how weak Helen was and at times disoriented. But showing Bill how much she cared despite her own suffering, well, that was Helen to the very end.

David drove from Georgia to Pittsburgh after Helen was rushed to Mercy Hospital in June 2014. He made it home just in time. One of the last things Helen said was, "David, give me a hug." When David was in combat overseas, Helen always said that she wished he was close enough for her to hug him.

She died shortly after getting a final hug from David.

Helen's influence on her kids endures because of who she was at the core.

"My mom really had a servant's heart," Kathy said.

That sensibility is what made her the perfect mother to help care for Dan after his accident.

Nothing better epitomized the job that Helen did battling cancer than the scene John Varoscak walked into one day when he visited the Priatkos. Dan had recently returned home for good from Harmarville Rehabilitation Center and Helen was working with him on his walking.

She had set up blocks in the foyer and told him, "Danny, we've got to go one block at a time." Helen stood behind him with her hand on his shoulder as Dan slowly took one step and then another. Nothing said motherly love to Varoscak more than what he saw that day.

"I'll never forget it," Varoscak said. "If I hadn't gone into the house, I never would have known Helen, who's fighting cancer, was able to help her son rehab."

One of Helen's biggest concerns before she passed was wondering who would take care of Dan. Bill assured her that she had done a wonderful job and that he and the kids would take care of Dan.

He told her that it was okay to let go.

Bill struggled with some guilt after Helen's death. The cancer had so ravaged her body that Helen couldn't eat toward the end. Bill implored her to try so she could keep up her strength. Had he pushed too hard? He asked himself that question a lot before receiving a vision one night.

He was in their bedroom when he saw Helen dressed in a blue dress. She told him she was with Jesus. She said Bill needed to live for Jesus and the kids until they were all together again.

It gave Bill an overwhelming sense of peace, and his guilt disappeared when that vision left him.

Even in death, Helen managed to comfort her loved ones.

Henry Heer still remembers the time Bill Priatko left him speechless.

The two were at California State College for the 1970-71 school year, Bill as an assistant dean of men and Heer as a student and residence assistant at McCloskey Hall. One night, he was working at the front desk of the dormitory and asked Bill, who was nearby in his office, what he was doing.

Bill said he was reading a letter from his friend Bart Starr. Heer thought he was kidding. Bill showed him the letter, which prompted the only question that could be asked: "How in the heck do you know Bart Starr?"

Green Bay Packers legend Bart Starr with David, Dan, and Bill at Packers
training camp when Starr was the team's head coach.

Bill didn't play long in the NFL, but he sure made a lasting impression. And not just on Starr, the Pro Football Hall of Fame quarterback
who won the first two Super Bowls in NFL history.

The Steelers selected Bill to represent the 1950s when they celebrated their 80th anniversary in 2012. He sat next to Joe Greene, at
"Mean Joe's" request, for the 80th anniversary team picture, and was on
the field at halftime against the Baltimore Ravens when the team was
honored. Not bad for a kid from North Braddock.

His greatest athletic moment received an exclamation point when
Bill received a standing ovation after his speech at a banquet for the nine-
teen honorees.

Bill sits next to "Mean" Joe Greene in a photo of players representing the
Steelers for their 80th anniversary celebration in 2012.

"We may not have had the salaries they have today," Bill said in closing
his speech, "but my greatest honor was to wear the Black 'N Gold for a
wonderful man, 'The Chief,' Mr. Art Rooney, Sr."

As with the Rooneys, one of the first families in professional football, Bill made lasting friendships with some of the game's biggest names.
He counted among his good friends Chuck Noll, Paul Brown, and Starr,
whom he met when he spent time with the Green Bay Packers in 1957.

Dick LeBeau is his closest friend, and the two talk at least once a
week on the phone. LeBeau, in fact, made a trip to North Braddock
in July 2019 to take part in a roundtable discussion among western
Pennsylvania high school football coaches. The attendees are a Who's
Who of the region's prep football coaches with scores of WPIAL and

state championships among them. Bill, of course, is friends with all the coaches, and he presides over the annual gathering that he started.

When Bill asked LeBeau to attend the roundtable, LeBeau accepted the invitation, even though he had to drive from Cincinnati to Pittsburgh and back in the same day.

Bill and Dick LeBeau at Pittsburgh Steelers training camp in Latrobe, Pennsylvania

Bill has that effect on people, which is why he had to play amateur detective one time. It came after he received an envelope with $500. It was for the admission fee that David had to pay to West Point. Bill had no idea who sent it, so he started asking around.

John Varoscak finally owned up to the good deed. He told Bill that he simply wanted to do something nice because of all that Bill had done for him.

Such a gesture wouldn't have surprised Dr. Roger Fischer.

Fischer, a former Pennsylvania state representative and Protestant minister, and Bill served in the Air Force Reserves together. Bill always wrote him letters, asking about his sons when they were in the army and stationed in Iraq. And, of course, Bill was there when Fischer officially became an ordained minister.

"Bill has always been very loyal and very caring," Fischer said. "He feels a genuine unity with you. He's like your brother and your best friend all rolled into one."

That sentiment led Fischer to the Priatko house in May 2013.

He had felt bad because he couldn't attend Bill's induction into the Western Chapter of the Pennsylvania Sports Hall of Fame. He apologized to Bill and handed him a congratulatory plaque that he and his wife, Kitty, had made. Bill's eyes misted as he cradled the plaque and read the inscription:

- An extremely faithful servant of God with Christ in the Holy Spirit who was and is
- A 2013 inductee into the Western Chapter of the Pennsylvania Sports Hall of Fame
- A very devoted man in love with his wife and family
- An outstanding professional football player and athlete
- A dedicated military officer and patriot
- A superb mentor, exemplar, and teacher of young people
- A magnificent caregiver
- A wonderful friend and uplifter
- A kind, wise, and sagacious gentleman

The fifth line explains why Bill made lifelong friends with Henry Heer and Mike Siyufy while all three were at California State College. Heer and Siyufy, who were residence assistants when Bill served as a dean of students, both consider him family.

"He's been more of a positive role model to me than my father and my two older brothers," said Siyufy, a retired teacher. "Whenever I'm having a problem or going through a tough time, he's the person I call. He listens and then gives me great advice."

Tim Tracy played defensive back for Bill at California State and also stays in regular contact with him. He was among the former players who insisted that Bill join them for a reunion at a 2019 California University football game. Of course, he did.

"You can probably count on one hand the people who don't like Bill Priatko," said Tracy, who is in the school's athletic Hall of Fame. "And if they don't like Bill Priatko, you probably need to get away from them because there's something wrong with them."

Kristy Dubinsky gravitated to Bill when she was a three-sport athlete at Yough High School and he served as its athletic director. They stayed in touch after Dubinsky went to college and later in her job as an art teacher at Elizabeth Forward High School.

She has met Dan several times and was so moved by his story that she expressed it through art. Dubinsky carved a cross out of wood with a chainsaw and didn't stop there. She painted an American flag draped on the cross to symbolize Dan's passion for West Point and his faith. The cross hangs on the game room wall of the Priatko home, right next to a sketch that Bob Weaver drew for Dan.

Weaver, who does illustrations for Pittsburgh author Jim O'Brien's sports books, took a collection of pictures that Bill gave him and turned them into a drawing. It shows Dan in various stages of his life, including as a cadet.

The cross that Kristy Dubinsky made for Dan hangs next to Bob
Weaver's drawing.

Having the odes to Dan side by side is especially meaningful to
Bill since Weaver taught Dubinsky at Yough. That he is close with
both teacher and pupil reflects the kind of relationships that Bill forges
with people.

"We could just talk for hours and get lost in conversation about sports
and things like that," Dubinsky said. "The way he's able to connect with
people is amazing."

Indeed, Bill seems straight out of *Mister Rogers' Neighborhood*. He
is Mr. Rogers, without the sweater. That comes back to something Bill's
mother always told her children: be kind to people. Bill combined that
with his abiding belief to love others as God loves us. Not surprisingly,
his list of friends might be thicker than a phone book.

"There's a reason why he knows everybody," said Tom Stabile, a former
NFL referee who became friends with Bill through former WPIAL executive director and NFL referee Charles "Ace" Heberling. "Bill is the kind
of guy who makes you feel more important than anybody on the face
of the earth."

Heberling agreed.

"I don't have any friends better than Bill," Heberling said a couple of months before he died in December 2019. "He doesn't miss a trick if it's your birthday or if you're getting an award. I've known a lot of people in the athletic field, and Bill Priatko and Dan have to be in the top three."

E rnie Furno still remembers driving past Norwin Stadium after Dan had started walking again. He rarely passed it without seeing Dan and Bill on the football field.

"Rain or shine, (Dan) would walk from one end and back, and his dad would be behind him one step up to the next step," said Furno, who owns Mr. Mike's Pizza Pub in Irwin. "It didn't matter what day of the week it was or what time it was, they were there every day for years."

That serves as the perfect metaphor for Bill and Dan. Bill has been behind Dan in every way that a father can. That is especially true following the accident.

Carol Bush has a unique perspective on their father-son relationship. She has never known one without the other as she worked in the Army football ticket office when Dan started returning to West Point for games. Carol would help Bill with tickets and parking, and a friendship blossomed between Bush and the Priatkos.

She met Dan shortly after his accident when he was confined to a wheelchair. She was struck by how happy and cheerful he was when he returned to West Point for the first time.

Bush saw the progress that Dan made, from the early years when he insisted on standing up, before getting what Bush calls "their annual photo," to Dan walking to his seat in Michie Stadium. She couldn't believe the first time she saw Dan stand up with Bill's help. She was just as floored the first time she saw Dan climb the stadium steps to his seat.

"It's an amazing story that he can function at the level he does," Bush said. "I would think Dan is a miracle, but he is also driven by Bill. He has this strength. I don't know where he gets it from. Both of them."

Dan with Carol Bush at an Army football game in West Point

Bush retired in 2014 after working thirty-five years in the football ticket office and Army's athletic office. She stays in touch with Dan and Bill and, of course, still sees them when they visit West Point for a game.

"They've touched my life and, I'm sure, so many other people's lives, too," Bush said. "Maybe the thing that was so impressive was their everything-is-possible attitude and the relationship between them."

That relationship has all the trappings of a typical father-son bond. Bill and Dan watch football together, share a weakness for chocolate (and Wendy's Baconator fries), and joke around with one another.

The two shared a memorable night in February 2016, one punctuated at the end of it with Dan's humor.

Bill was inducted into the Robert Morris Athletic Hall of Fame and the emotions it stirred went beyond Bill getting immortalized by the school. Hall of Fame emcee Chris Shovlin, the longtime radio voice of the Robert Morris football and basketball teams, relayed a story right before calling Bill to the stage to give his acceptance speech. Earlier that day, Shovlin told the crowd, he had received a phone call from Nashville, Tennessee.

"I said to myself, 'Who in the heck is calling me from Nashville? Am I getting an audition for the Grand Ole Opry?'" said Shovlin, who had been inducted into the school's athletic Hall of Fame three years earlier.

The crowd laughed and Shovlin revealed that he was just as flabbergasted when the caller turned out to be Dick LeBeau, who was in his second year as the Tennessee Titans' defensive coordinator. LeBeau had planned on attending the induction ceremony but couldn't make it because of a staff meeting. He asked Shovlin if he would do him a favor and deliver a message at the induction dinner: "Please convey that I'm so proud of Bill and happy for him and his induction into the Robert Morris Hall of Fame."

If that surprise from his dearest friend wasn't enough to make Bill's eyes a little misty, consider what happened later.

The 1994 Robert Morris softball team, which won the last of four consecutive Northeast Conference Championships, was inducted, and Monica Everett spoke on behalf of that squad. During her speech, she cited Bill and said his impact on her was so profound that she had gone into the ministry.

"Mr. P, you indicated that you are so grateful to be inducted as an administrator since you weren't a player or a coach," she said. "You may not be inducted as a player or a coach, but the positive influence you have had on my life and my teammates from our days as student-athletes at Robert Morris to this very day, we will appreciate forever."

The drive home gave Bill time to process the emotions of the evening and reflect a little. He had already been inducted into the Western Pennsylvania and East Boros Sports Halls of Fame and was pushing his mid-eighties. He said to Dan, "This will probably be the last award I win."

Bill could not have set up Dan any better.

"No, Dad," Dan said, "you'll be the Resident of the Month in a nursing home."

He and Bill both cracked up.

D r. William Kerr, the superintendent of Norwin School District, was getting closer to retirement in 2017 and he wanted to do something for Dan. He created the Noble Knight Award and presented it to Dan during a school board meeting in the spring of that year.

"It's something that I felt was in my own heart because there are people in our lives that make such a great difference, and he continues to be that inspiration to many," said Kerr, who retired in 2019. "Dan Priatko exemplifies all the attributes of good character. His story is remarkable, and it's one the needs to be shared with others."

Kerr spread the story whenever he could. He and Norwin High School principal Michael Choby had Dan speak to about 500 district employees before the start of the 2017 school year. Sam Glenn, a well-known inspirational speaker, was the keynote speaker, but Dan carried the room with the message that was as resonant as it was timeless.

"When I came out of my coma and realized what I now was, my attitude was tested," Dan said in the auditorium of his alma mater. "Do I moan and groan and say, 'Why me?' Or do I accept what I now am? My attitude was strengthened by the words in Philippians in my West Point Bible: 'I have learned to be content whatever the circumstances.' I have taken an attitude of gratitude that I am still here and can do the best I can to help others. I have faith that when I when I get to Heaven, I will have a new body."

Dan received a standing ovation after his talk. His sister, Kathy, was among those who wiped away tears.

Bill couldn't attend the event that day because he was at Tennessee Titans training camp visiting Dick LeBeau, the Titans' defensive coordinator. But he received a handful of emails while in Nashville about Dan. One of them came from Colleen Weaver, a Norwin teacher and the wife of Bob Weaver.

"Sam Glenn was excellent and very inspiring, but, to be honest, the few words that Dan spoke were even more inspirational because he lives his life with the 'perfect attitude' under very difficult circumstances," Weaver wrote to Bill the day of hearing Dan. "As tears filled my eyes, I told myself to have a positive and grateful attitude not only throughout this school year but throughout my life. I know how proud you are of Dan, but this moment today would have added to your pride."

Another email came from Norwin girls' volleyball coach Mary Ellen Ferragonio.

"I wanted to tell you that we were so blessed to have your Dan and your very beautiful daughter at our in-service meetings the other day," Ferragonio wrote. "The introduction Mr. Choby gave for Dan was wonderful and very heartfelt, and Dan's message of attitude, hope, and trust was one we all need to hear (again and again and again!). You have an amazing family and this community is so lucky to have your family as a part of it."

Those emails reflect the effect Dan has on people.

"I've never heard Dan Priatko complain because he continues to have that trust in God, faith in the beliefs that he has, and faith in other people," Kerr said. "Dan is a living, breathing epitome of what it means to refuse to give up, to fight for what's right."

Dan knew no other way, which is why the late Don Kattic made a point of attending the school board meeting at which Dan was presented the Noble Knight Award. Kattic was a local institution. A beloved history teacher for years at Norwin High School, he had served in the Korean War with the Marines. Nobody did more to champion those who had served their country than Kattic.

He was the Veterans of Foreign Wars (VFW) Commander in Irwin/North Huntingdon for two decades and oversaw the construction and restoration of veterans memorials. He also organized and led Memorial and Veterans Day parades and ceremonies for years.

"I am so appreciative to be here," Kattic said the night Dan received the Noble Knight Award, "to see a man honored who I deeply love and respect. He is special. I admire him for his spirit, faith, courage, and patriotism."

Dan's Noble Knight Award was the first of an impressive and unprecedented hat trick. In 2018, he was inducted into the Norwin Athletic Hall of Fame. He also received a Distinguished Alumni Award from Norwin that year.

Norwin Athletic Hall of Fame committee member Darryl Bertani wrote a tribute to Dan before his induction. Here is part of it:

Courage can be exhibited in a variety of ways. Obviously, it is found on a battlefield, and it is also on display in sports and everyday life. No matter where it occurs, courage has one common denominator, and that is adversity. Trying to overcome hardship requires special recognition.

Dan Priatko has been dealt one of life's cruelest fates, having become permanently disabled through a horrific accident. Yet, he has never given up and never will. He has stared misfortune in the eye, but he will never let it overcome him or define him.

He is a fighter teeming with willpower and determination, which serves him well in his daily endeavors. He is a prime example of someone who doesn't surrender despite the odds against him. For these reasons and for being a stellar athlete, scholar, and person, Dan Priatko is entering the Norwin Athletic Hall of Fame.

Bob "Bo" Garritano emceed the Hall of Fame and Distinguished Alumni dinners and said roughly half the tables for the Distinguished

Alumni dinner were filled by Dan's friends and family members. About a quarter of Dan supporters filled the tables at the Norwin Athletic Hall of Fame dinner.

"You couldn't get enough of what he said," Garritano said.

Craig Wolfley agreed. The former Pittsburgh Steelers offensive lineman and current sideline reporter for Steelers radio broadcasts has a son, Kyle, who graduated from West Point, served in Afghanistan and teaches at West Point. "Dan's gratefulness to West Point warmed my heart," he said after hearing Dan's acceptance speech.

Dan flanked by former Norwin High School football teammates Ernie Furno and Frank Klanchar after a 2018 dinner honoring Dan and other inductees of the Norwin Athletic Hall of Fame. The three were tri-captains in 1979.

Nancy Bush, who had been a Norwin class officer with Dan, drove from outside of Washington, D.C., to the Hall of Fame dinner. She simply wanted to be there for Dan.

Joe Ravasio and Marcus McCullough were also in attendance. Ravasio is the former Ringgold High School football coach who had Dan speak to his team in 1987. McCullough was one of the captains from that team. McCullough had been captivated when he heard Dan speak, and he used Dan's message of perseverance as motivation. Seeing Dan again confirmed to McCullough that what Dan had said more than thirty years earlier was anything but empty talk.

"I was like, 'Wow, he's really living his words,'" said McCullough, who works at East Allegheny High School and coaches football there. "People can lie. People can pretend. This guy here is no pretender."

Dorothy Tragesser, Dan's former speech therapist, understands better than most how difficult it was for Dan to speak at his Hall of Fame induction. She was like a proud teacher when he nailed his speech.

"It's such an effort for him to speak clearly at an event like that and he gave the most eloquent speech," Tragesser said. "Everyone in the room understood exactly what he was saying."

No one who was honored with Dan at the Distinguished Alumni Award banquet understood him better than former U.S. Congressman Mark Critz. Dan and Critz went back to middle school and were a lot alike. Each was driven, goal-oriented, and prone to the occasional goofing around.

They played football together, and Dan impressed Critz with how he made himself into a player. He was never the biggest guy and certainly not the fastest guy, but Dan willed himself into becoming a starting running back, a team captain, and team MVP as a senior. Looking back, Critz sees that time as a portal into the resolve that Dan needed after the accident that probably should have left him barely functional.

Critz gained even more of an appreciation for Dan when he served as a U.S. Congressman. Critz was always extremely impressed by the resumes and recommendations he sifted through when weighing potential appointments to military academies. They were the best of the best. It impressed upon him how difficult it is to gain admission to a military academy.

Dan had not only gotten into West Point, he had graduated with honors, distinguished himself as a battalion commander, and become an Army Ranger. That and what Dan accomplished following his accident made getting a Distinguished Alumni Award with Dan one of the proudest moments of Critz's life.

As he accepted the award, Critz said, "I am honored to be a Distinguished Alumni and my greatest honor is to be inducted with Dan Priatko." He later elaborated on why he had said that.

"He's made me, I don't know a better person but a stronger person," said Critz, who works as an advisor to Pennsylvania Governor Tom Wolf on rural development and policy. "I think about those things when I'm down. He's one of the inspirations I look to say, 'Okay, step up, Mark, and do what you can. And don't stop.' I don't know if there's anyone who couldn't be inspired by someone who persevered through (his accident) and then continued living his life and doing what he could to improve his physical life but also remaining true to who he is — someone who makes sure that whatever he is doing, he is contributing to the community."

To Critz, Dan is an inspirational movie come to life.

Rudy is an apt comparison because the protagonist of that popular movie was considered too small and too slow before he made Notre Dame's football team as a walk-on. Where Dan goes beyond *Rudy* is what he has overcome since his accident.

"Not to downplay Rudy's achievements, but if you compare (his story) to what Dan's been through, I think it pales in comparison," Critz said. "It's interesting because Rudy's this famous character, this famous person, this famous movie, and I'm thinking to myself, 'Oh my goodness, Dan has persevered through so much more.' Year after year, day after day, hour after hour, he just keeps at it."

As an Army Ranger does.

All the way and then some.
That is Dan.

A book of Dan wouldn't be complete without his words. He has always been a terrific writer, and that is one gift his accident never took from him. Dan regularly emails friends and family members and writes poetry. Two of his best poems are odes to Bill and Helen, the two most important people in his life.

Dan wrote this one year for Father's Day:
I thought and pondered and mused late into the night
Hoping that I could find words to describe Dad just right
We all know praiseworthy traits in surplus do abound
People past and present extolling Dad are plenty to be found
For though Dad has accomplished much good in his life.
From education to athletics to marrying a wonderful wife
Along the way came four siblings who are thankful for Dad
Health care, military service, and education are very glad
Those children did multiply to grace us with four sweethearts
Dear grandchildren each with an angelic face just for starts
And the work ethic that Dad teaches and lives of giving your all
Enables his children in their vocational lives to stand tall
Over the years Dad's sacrifices for his family were so many
All to care for our well-being and earn a pretty penny
Dad knows strong faith and trust in our Lord are the key
To true and lasting success the best formula we will see
Yes, the ninth verse of Psalm Twenty-Five teaches us all
An invaluable, timeless truth when we faithfully heed His call
The meek will He guide in judgement and show them His way

Dad, may God bless you with a most joyful Father's Day!

Bob Weaver, a close family friend, drew this portrait of Dan, Bill, and Helen in December 2019.

Dan wrote this about his mother shortly after she died:

As people all around the world honor their mothers both past and present
Our hearts cherish the blessing of Mom preciously touching our lives each day,

Her unselfish and sacrificial presence was a beautiful gift from our
loving Lord
Mom's heart overflowed with love, understanding, and patience too
often to say.
We were blessed perhaps more than we knew, what a true gem our
family had
For etched in our hearts and ingrained in our minds are invaluable
lessons galore,
Taught not only by words but by humble and quiet example Mom
impacted our lives
She prepared us for school days and vacations along with dutiful
housekeeping and more.
The "dutiful housekeeping" was not only maintaining the cleanliness
of our home at 12378
But cleaning other homes transpired to aid her husband in working
extra jobs to earn cash,
Mom, your offspring offer thanks to you for sweet and fond memo-
ries treasured in our hearts
So that priceless recollections will come our way when our child-
hood ways we do rehash.
An integral part of those "recollections" and "memories" is groceries
strewed on the floor
Often faithful lady-friend neighbors would venture to transport
Mom to thriftily shop for food
For a vibrant and active family o'er the years seemingly insatiable
appetites would have
One can rest assured for Mom's tasty treats and delicious foods we
were always in the mood!
A special memory from our childhood days is nights when the card
club ladies did meet
Joyful laughter did fill the air as in friendship card hands were dealt
and snacks consumed,

A memory that is special, too, and precious indeed is Mom preparing
us to attend church
Rising early to ensure we were appropriately and properly attired and
fittingly groomed.
As children we grew and our activities became numerous and busy
schedules did vary
Color guard, football, raising volleyballs and our voices in song; the
routines were diverse,
Yet through it all from differing meal times to cleaning clothes Mom
stayed the course
With sacrifice, steadfastness, and perseverance, Mom was at our side
for better or worse.
Our post-high school years were diverse with collegiate experiences
of varying degrees
Community College to the Long Gray Line to the towering
Cathedral of Learning at Pitt,
Loving Mom was supportive with a tasty homecoming meal of foods
close to the heart
We knew in our soul come high tide or low that with Mom we would
have the perfect fit.
Upon bidding farewell to our Rockbound Highland Home at West
Point duty does call
Deployment four times of her beloved son to war in the Mid-East
did try Mom's soul,
Yet as a lifetime of unwavering faith in Jesus Christ with a heart of
strength had shown
Through trials and tribulations of every kind Mom would assume the
steadfast rock role.
From Air Force duties to athletics to teaching and more the family
patriarch stood tall
Long hours and distances through the years, including working
nights to make ends meet,

A consensus from dear Mom of blessed memory and a grateful and
growing family
For loyalty, integrity, and time-proven love for us all the head of our
family can't be beat.
A "growing family" for which Grandma's devoted love for her grandchildren knew no end
Yes, Kurtis, Michaela, Kristopher, and David are the current and
unfading stars of the show,
Nurturing their numerous athletic, acting, singing talents, and
untold more diverse skills
Pride, love, and contentment in her grandmother's heart Mom did
constantly feel we know.
True, special, and lasting friendships along the road of life are sure to
come our way
Good friends are like family we cherish and enjoy through visits,
phone calls, and mail.
Mom through her past experience at work had established one such
dear and loyal friend
Through matrimony faithful friend Ilenor united with Richard to
assume the surname of Nale.
I offer great thanks as one who has been the recipient of Mom's
loving devotion and understanding
Her sacred bond of love, compassion, and servanthood established
o'er the years will never sever,
Dad, Debbie, Dave, Dottie, Keith, Kathy, Michaela, Kurtis, David,
Kristopher, all family and friends agree
Our beloved Mom and Grandma is alive in our grateful hearts and
souls <u>ALWAYS and FOREVER!!!</u>

EPILOGUE

Dan Priatko rides a motorized scooter through Redstone Highlands Assisted Living Facility on a spectacular May day. He is wearing navy blue slacks (navy, Dan?), a blue shirt matching the cloudless sky outside, and a watch. Of course, it is set to military time.

While making his regular rounds at the North Huntingdon senior care home, he stops in Irene Kifus's room. After they exchange pleasantries, Dan asks Kifus if she watched the Kentucky Derby over the weekend. He then reaches for the clipboard in the front basket of his scooter. He scans the page clipped to the board and asks Kifus if she knows that Cheerios' original name was CheeriOats and that *Odd Couple* was a movie before it was a hit TV show.

Dan mines newspapers, the Almanac, radio, and TV for such factoids, writing them down for work. They help him engage the residents and are emblematic of how seriously Dan takes his job, even though he isn't paid a penny for doing it.

All the way and then some. Dan still lives by the Army Rangers motto.

After visiting Kifus, Dan motors outside where a group of residents are enjoying the sun. The residents are afflicted with dementia or Alzheimer's Disease. One woman in a wheelchair is inconsolable and repeatedly cries out for her brother. Dan sits next to her and pats her hand reassuringly.

These patients hold a special place in Dan's heart since one of his favorite high school teachers is dealing with similar issues. Jeanne Close was Dan's chorus teacher at Norwin High School. They remained close after he graduated. After Dan's accident, Close paid tribute to Dan by having the chorus sing "Danny Boy" at its spring show. Close no longer recognizes Dan, but he always makes sure to visit with her.

"He holds her hand, and she knows that it is someone special in her life," said Kate Smith, a care partner at Redstone. "Dan is so special because he visits with every single person in our Personal Care and Memory Care. He has a personal relationship with each one of them. He just uplifts everybody."

Smith looks forward to Dan's work shifts as much as her patients. Getting to know him has made her a better person.

"His attitude is 'I can do it, no matter what. Whatever circumstances come my way, I'm going to overcome it,'" Smith said. "If I'm having a bad day, I think about him. I can't have a bad day if he's coming in my door. He puts it in perspective."

Smith's mother, Lisa, also works as a care partner and she said Dan fills a critical role at Redstone. Lisa Smith said some of the residents don't have much family or have family members who are unable to visit regularly.

"People need somebody to spend time with them and care about them," Lisa Smith said. "That's what Dan provides."

She looks forward to Dan coming through the sliding glass doors at Redstone as much as her daughter. That puts them in the same company as everyone at Redstone, where Dan is a veritable celebrity because of his positive attitude.

"How can you be in that position and always have a smile on your face?" Lisa Smith said. "I don't know if I could do that. Rain or shine, he's here. With a smile. With a joke. All of that."

K ate Smith became friends with Dan at Redstone, but she first met him at Planet Fitness in North Huntingdon.

One day she noticed a man moving slowly from machine to machine and using a quad cane. She wondered if she should try to help him. When she posed that question to a girl at the front desk, she was told, "No, you'll offend him."

Smith approached Dan that day but only to thank him for providing an example with his determination.

Dan is as much a regular at Planet Fitness as he is at Redstone. Bill drops him off and picks him up three to four days a week. Just like at Redstone, people look forward to seeing Dan at Planet Fitness. Everybody seems to know him—or at least who he is.

One time his sister Debbie was working out at Planet Fitness at the same time as Dan. They talked for a bit before Dan resumed his regimen. A man approached Debbie and asked if she knew Dan. She told him he is her brother.

"You're kidding!" the man said. "He is amazing!"

Tom Stabile thought the same thing the time he saw Dan walking into Planet Fitness.

"You couldn't open the door for him," said Stabile, a longtime friend of Bill's. "I was just so amazed at how dedicated he was and just how he conducted his life."

Dan's approach to life reminds fellow West Pointer Tom Abraham of his former college roommate.

"He lost a leg in Vietnam and, over the years, he gradually went downhill because of Agent Orange and it was a neurological disease he had that was like Parkinson's," said Abraham, who lives in Unity Township, Pennsylvania. "The guy never said that there's something he can't do. He ran marathons. He skied. He played me in racquetball and he has a prosthetic leg. He never felt sorry for himself and he never blamed anybody else. That's pretty much the way Danny is, and that's a West Point thing."

Abraham served in Vietnam and befriended Bill when the latter was on the Air Force flight crew that transported him to Southeast Asia. In 2018, Abraham started Veteran Angels, a non-denominational organization that helps traumatized veterans suffering through spiritual healing. Abraham has considered inviting Dan to one of its retreats as a speaker.

"When he's on his game and making a speech, you look at him and see how positive he is," Abraham said. "I don't think there's any Wounded Warriors that would walk away from that feeling sorry for themselves."

Dan's biggest strength, his unbending resolve, is also what worries his family as he gets older.

He does not allow anyone to help him get out of a car or sometimes even hold open a door for him. Do it and you will get a polite but firm "no thank you." What makes Dan so authentic is that he acts this way even in the privacy of his home. A family member who trails him too closely in case he starts to fall will be told to back off. That is all part of Dan refusing to make any concessions to his condition and encroaching age.

"I always tell him, 'Dan, people are trying to be nice, trying to help you,'" Bill said. "He just wants to be independent."

Dan's refusal of help is his way of asserting control, independence even, over the catastrophic accident that stole so much from him. He knows he has limitations, but he refuses to cede any ground to them.

In December 2019, Bill and Dan went to a viewing at a local funeral home. It would have taken Dan ten seconds to go in had he used his wheelchair. He insisted on walking, and it took close to ten minutes for Dan to get inside. Bill walked patiently with him the entire time.

Dan surprised his father a month later when they were driving to church and "I Need You Every Hour" started playing on the radio. The hymn about God took Dan back to the day when he was getting an evaluation at Walter Reed Military Medical Center, a year after his accident. Doctors concluded that Dan was permanently disabled and that he had to be medically discharged from active duty.

"While I was laying around waiting for my exam," he told his father, "I kept looking at the clock on the wall, and that hymn was deeply on my mind."

Bill had never heard that before.

W hen Kathy Camp looks back on it, she needed to see Dan that day in Michie Stadium.

As the daughter of Reverend Richard Camp, who served as Army's chaplain from 1973-96, Kathy had grown up in West Point. But when she returned for a football game in October 2019, it didn't feel like she had come home. Sure, the buildings and the barracks were the same, and the gameday experience was still second to none.

But she didn't know any of the people that had made West Point, well West Point, when she spent her formative years there. That is why something felt like it was missing until she spotted two men out of the corner of her eye.

Camp was walking out of the stadium after the game, and she initially didn't think anything of what she saw. But something compelled her to stop. She looked again and saw that it was Bill and Dan. The three shared a tearful reunion inside the stadium.

Kathy Camp finally felt like she was home.

"When I hugged Dan, I felt his wave of emotions, which then caused more waves of emotion for me," she said. "They are a team, and it's breathtaking."

Dan flanked by Bill and Kathy Camp at a 2019 Army football game in West Point. Photo courtesy of Kathy Camp.

Camp had been a little girl when Dan attended West Point. He became close with her family, and she looked at him through a big brother/hero lens. Dan's mystique grew when he spoke at a Thanksgiving church service in 1995. Camp, who was still an impressionable young girl, was in the pews that day. She watched in awe as cadets in their wool gray coats leaned forward so they could hear every word. Just as memorable to Camp was the standing ovation that Dan received as he walked back to his seat.

She stayed in touch with Dan through the years and still looks forward to getting letters or emails from him, especially with her father struggling because of Parkinson's disease.

"He's incredibly poetic with his words," said Camp, who lives in the Washington, D.C. area and owns a public relations firm. "He has both the intellect and the vocabulary to write really beautiful letters and then this emotional intelligence. It has no pain, it has no barriers, it has no ego, it has no reservations that most men have in their writing. All I can think of is that God's not through with him yet."

If Dan still inspires Camp, so does his family.

"How do you find hope in a hopeless situation? How do you grow old when you know that your child is dependent on you?" she said. "And they do it in a way that's really encouraging. You feel their joy. You feel their hope. You feel their love, and people who have perfectly, healthy, first-world lives don't have that. They have a plan, they have a mission, and in a way that I certainly don't have, and I'm healthy."

To West Point graduate and retired Major General Joseph Bergantz, the accident that changed everything in many ways, changed nothing in the most important ways. Dan and his family stayed true to who they are despite the most trying of circumstances.

"People are given situations sometimes that other people would say they don't deserve and they certainly could take it to the point where they say, 'Hey, I've been praying about this and it's not working,' and they would lose their faith and believe that God's not really listening to their prayers," Bergantz said. "But not Dan. Dan perseveres. Dan believes. He's got to be probably the most faithful believer I've ever met and his family."

Bergantz was a mentor to Dan at West Point and he and his wife, Helen, were the last two people to see Dan and Debbie before the accident. The two had stayed with the Bergantzes right before the accident.

"If all that had happened to me, I might not have been so understanding," said Bergantz, a retired Major General who lives in Huntsville, Alabama. "Dan never lets that drag him down, and Bill's the same way. It reminds me of the book of Job, the trial and tribulations that guy went through but he hung in there."

The accident revealed what has always been Dan's core—and that goes beyond sheer grit and perseverance.

"He cares more about others, I think, than himself, and he loves everybody," Bergantz said. "That's the way we all ought to be."

AFTERWORD

As I contemplate how my life-changing car accident has affected me and my life, it is the reality of THE POWER OF PRAYER!!! I have come to the realization and acceptance of the fact that, in and of myself, I fall short. Granted, my extensive physical and mental training, be it athletic, military, academic, and much more, have proven an invaluable component of my inner being that has helped me to cope with my life-changing, traumatic brain injury. But, the prayers of so many people and the hands-on support of numerous individuals, including family, friends, church members and members from other church denominations, doctors, medical personnel, therapists, and so many others, have helped to sustain me. For that, I am so grateful.

When I became aware of my condition after my accident and with the heart-breaking realization that my path in life and my goals were now drastically changed, the verse in Philippians 3:14 strengthened me: "I press on toward the goal for the prize of the upward call of God in Christ Jesus." I had a decision to make. Should I complain and say WHY ME or should I do my best at whatever path in life that God has led me to? I chose the latter. I have found it to be rewarding in my volunteer position at Redstone Highlands Assisted Living Facility where I do my best to bring a smile to the residents when I visit their rooms.

My adversity and my faith have taught me to focus less on my disabled condition and more on Jesus Christ and what His will is for me. A positive attitude toward handling adversity is a helpful attribute.

However, a positive, God-centered attitude toward handling adversity is more effective than a self-centered attitude, as it provides greater hope. Most of all, when experiencing any trial in life, only by living the words of Psalm 37:4, which leaves with us the encouraging and reassuring truth of "Delight yourself in the Lord and he will give you the desires of your heart" and then "I can do all things through Christ who strengthens me." The words of Paul in Philippians 4:11 further sustain me: "I have learned to be content in whatever circumstances I am."

All the Bible verses provide a deep, abiding faith that whenever I get to heaven, I will have a new body.

—— Dan Priatko

W e always think and feel that a form of misfortune happens to others and not to us, until it hits us personally.

A phone call to my wife, Helen, and me at 5:20 p.m. on March 4, 1985, from our daughter, Debbie, from the Hazleton Hospital, hit us personally. Debbie's emotional words were short and painful: "We have been in an accident and the state trooper said Dan is fighting for his life." When Helen and I arrived at the hospital, the medical prognosis was bleak and never changed for the next eighteen months. We were told that Dan's injuries were irreversible. We never lost our faith that Dan would be what he once was, but we had to face the reality of God's will.

From that moment of Debbie's terse phone call, for days, weeks, months, and to this day, my family's lives revolved around supporting and loving one another and doing our best to accept what had happened to a son and brother who all of his life was as fine a young man that any parents and a family could hope for. From the time Dan came out of his long coma to this day, our family's sense of pride, love, and respect for Dan has strengthened us to where we thank God for what he now is and how he has handled his very difficult life.

I will candidly admit that when I stood by Dan's bedside in the Intensive Care Unit, as he battled for his life, I blamed myself for Dan's misfortune and his circumstances. I am not a saint and have fallen short in my life, absent from perfection with shortcomings. We know that God forgives our iniquities, but I felt that possibly I was being punished. I tried to overcome this feeling, and I read John 9:2 in the Bible. It says, "His disciples asked Him, Rabbi, who sinned, this man or his parents, that he would be born blind? Jesus answered, "It was neither this man sinned, nor his parents; but it was so that the works of God might be displayed in him." Dan quoted Philippians 1:12 a year or so after his accident which says, "My circumstances have turned out for the greater progress of the gospel." Only God himself knows if Dan's accident was His plan for Dan's circumstances to further proclaim the teachings of Jesus. All of this can be a spiritual blessing to all of us who are in in the middle of adversity where we feel guilt or self-blame. God is good.

We know that God works in ways that we cannot sometimes comprehend, but we know He is never wrong. What I say next reveals God's presence in our lives. To my children and me, Helen was a saint. After almost thirty years of chemotherapy treatment for cancer, our Lord called her home. She did all she could in her wonderful, compassionate, caring ways to take care of Dan, from the day he was born and deeply so after Dan's accident. Helen's last several months were tough days when she couldn't eat, always saying she was trying but just couldn't. My children and I kept urging her to eat, and I pushed her to do so.

Thirty-three days after Helen passed away, I was lying in bed in the middle of the night, wide awake, in our darkened bedroom. I said out loud, "Honey, I feel so bad that I kept pushing you to eat, I wish I could talk to you." All of the sudden, Helen was standing there in the blue dress she wore at our 50th wedding anniversary dinner. She had a glowing light all around her. Her face was beautiful and radiant. She said, "Forget everything, I am with Jesus. Live for Jesus, for me, for Debbie, Dan, David, and Kathy, until we are all together again." I tried to reach out to her and she disappeared. I couldn't believe what I saw. It had to be seen to believe it. I know in my heart our Lord was helping to put my mind at ease. Most importantly, my family and I know where Helen is.

The beautiful, awesome scene that night will stay with me until we are all together again.

———- Bill Priatko

APPENDIX

Dan is a prolific writer, whether it is poetry, speeches, or letters and emails. Here are some of his writings:

Dan's Thanksgiving speech to West Point cadets in 1995

I n the dictionary, thanksgiving is defined as an expression of gratitude, especially to God. God has used adversity in my life to make me more thankful for everything that I do have. During my days here at the Academy, I knew the significance of right and wrong in our cadet relationships through the Cadet Honor Code. More than ever, I am grateful what I have gained through my accident and the strength our Lord has given me.

I am thankful for my upbringing, to include my family life, the high school I attended, and a father and mother who raised me in a God-fearing home. I am so grateful I came to West Point to be part of the Long Gray Line. I am thankful for the mental and physical disciplines that were instilled in me. I drew upon these quite often during my battle to win back my abilities to walk and talk and other rehabilitation efforts. What compels me to do more of an exercise than I have been instructed to do is the instinct to go above and beyond the call of duty. When fatigue would try to take over, making it easier to alibi, I remembered the words from the Cadet Prayer of choosing the harder right over the easier wrong.

My gratitude extends to the years I spent as an Army football player. The perseverance that I learned helped me so much in adapting to a changed lifestyle over the past ten years. I was often motivated by the words of Coach Jim Young when he said, "What the mind can conceive, the body can achieve." I am very thankful to be speaking here tonight in the Cadet Chapel. I am so appreciative for the spiritual training I received here during my years at the Academy and the leadership and support provided by Chaplain Camp and his staff. The spiritual training has continued to be a great help to me since those days.

The morning after my accident, the Corps of Cadets, at breakfast in Washington Hall, bowed their heads in prayer for my recovery. I am thankful for those prayers and countless others, including those from the West Point community. The kindness and mercy of God was and is shown through the power of prayer. God answering prayer was apparent in the job I now hold, serving as a recreation aide in a nursing home. In addition to the fact that beginning a job after sustaining a head injury is difficult, the West Point and Ranger attitude in me faced a real challenge in adjusting to my inability to do things. In frustration, I poured out my heart to the Lord one night. The answer was simple and straightforward: Just do your best! Now, I enjoy delivering mail in my motor cart. And I have gone from yelling out battalion orders to calling out Bingo numbers. The Lord has shown me that if we trust in Him, He will lead us in all that we are going through.

I lean heavily on the words of **Paul in Philippians 4:11 when he says, "NOT THAT I SPEAK FROM WANT: FOR I HAVE LEARNED TO BE CONTENT IN WHATEVER CIRCUMSTANCES I AM."** I am thankful for these things from the bottom of my heart, but THIS is what I am most thankful for. This is my West Point Bible that was issued during my Plebe Year and is symbolic of what I am most thankful for, the Word of God. During my years at the Academy, this Bible was the source of my strength. Since my accident and the day I came out of my coma, the Word of God has more than ever been the source of my strength, peace, and hope!

The night before I left my home for my trip to West Point the weekend of my accident, I read my West Point Bible. I highlighted the last verse that I read and left a marker on that page. It was **Philippians 4:13, I CAN DO ALL THINGS THROUGH CHRIST WHO STRENGTHENS ME.** After coming out of my coma, and every day since, Philippians 4:13 has been the cornerstone of my faith.

God bless each and every one of you! Have a wonderful Thanksgiving! When we all sit down at our tables on Thanksgiving Day, may we feel in our hearts **Psalm 92:1. IT IS GOOD TO GIVE THANKS TO THE LORD.**

Dan's speech to the Jacksonville Jaguars in 1996

P laying football has been a major part of my life. At West Point, I was a placekicker on the Army football team. During my days as a cadet, I attended Airborne School and, after graduation, completed U.S. Army Ranger School. I have gone from playing football and jumping out of airplanes to now working part-time in recreation at a nursing home. My life has drastically changed. I have gone from yelling military orders to calling out Bingo numbers. Following my accident, for more than a year, my only food intake was through a tube in my stomach.

As the reality of my accident settled in, I faced a choice: I could become bitter and depressed, wondering, "Why me?" Or I could lead each day to the best of my ability, trusting in Jesus Christ to be my source of peace and strength. Fortunately, I chose trusting in the Lord. And in doing so, I have come to live and feel Philippians 4:11: "Not that I speak from want, for I have learned to be content in whatever circumstances I am." And I have come to understand also that, as we are told in Philippians 1:12, "The things which have happened unto me have turned out for the greater progress of the Gospel."

Three years after my accident, I was speaking to a group of high school students at a Sunday school class. One student asked me if it bothered me to know I had such a promising career ahead of me shattered by my car accident. I responded by telling her that if my accident causes anyone to draw closer to Jesus Christ, I am glad my accident happened. And to you, I will express the same thought and will also state with all sincerity that my accident has brought me closer to Christ.

I was fortunate, and you have the opportunity to play the greatest game in the world—football. No other game reflects life the way football does. The values we learn from football can help us in life. We sometimes experience the agony of defeat, and few emotions can equal the elation of victory. As in life, we have to rebound after a defeat and face tomorrow. In your case, facing a new tomorrow is mentally and physically preparing to meet a new opponent the following week. The mental toughness so essential in football is also integral in leading a successful life.

As I came out of my seventh-month coma, the mental toughness that I learned from football was very helpful in my battle to regain functions that I once took for granted. I now had to dedicate myself to daily struggles to once again be able to walk, talk, and eat. Although mental toughness was important, it wasn't enough.

When I was a plebe at West Point, all new cadets were given this Bible. This was a continuation of a tradition that has lasted over 100 years. During my four years at the Academy, I relied upon my Bible. The night before my accident, I was reading my Bible and highlighted a verse: Philippians 4:13. I left a marker on that page and closed my Bible. Over seven months later, when I came out of my coma and gradually became aware of what happened to me, I was informed of my highlighting Philippians 4:13 the night before my accident. That verse has become the cornerstone of my faith in my continual battle to overcome adversity. As we are told in Philippians 4:13: "I can do all things through Christ who strengthens me."

That verse and all the words of the Lord have sustained me. As tough as we think we are, only Jesus Christ gives us true strength. May we be grateful for the mental toughness we have learned from football but more grateful for the peace and strength that come from Jesus Christ.

May our Lord give each one of you the strength to do well in your challenge tomorrow and all of your challenges, on and off the field.

Dan's poem in celebration of St. Nicholas Orthodox Church 100-year anniversary, dedicated to his mother, in 2016

As one scans the proud skyline of Donora, a prominent feature catches the eye,
A church with onion-shaped, blueish-green domes projecting toward the sky.
Grandparents and parents, the founders of our church,
Settled in the area and fulfilled their Christian Orthodox search.
Built with men of deep faith and strength with sweat and tears,
St. Nicholas Orthodox is a liturgical landmark that has stood for 100 years.
Where traditions and rich historical, spiritual legacies from the past are found,
"With faith, reverence and the fear of God," the faithful worship from all around.
Choir, Altar boys, Sunday School, Church Council, FOCA, St. Nicholas Society, Candle Room and more,
Loyal parishioners, all part of a great tradition of faith and service when they enter our church door.
The Very Reverend Father Igor Soroka shepherds, serves, and preaches to his flock to this day,

Along with visits by Church Hierarchs and brother clergy devotedly
showing the Way.
Joyful baptisms and weddings, to more solemn funerals, we have
been and are served well,
How continually blessed we all have been mere words cannot adequately express or tell.
A revered blessing, the eternal memory of Matushka Irene, spiritually
felt, every day,
Who served church and family in her compassionate and loving way.
We thank our Lord Jesus for our beloved church on the hill,
Which strengthens our Orthodox Christian faith through His
grace and will.

Dan's ode to former West Point chaplain Richard Camp

From Wheaton to West Point Chaplain Camp did embark
On a faithful spiritual journey of service to the Lord.
With a life showing strength, peace, joy, and love
Into each life he touched the Holy Spirit was poured.
On the banks of the Hudson sits our rockbound highland home
Of which Chaplain Camp became a vital part,
Over the years making it plain for all to see
To Jesus Christ and these gray walls he gave his very heart.
To all who accepted the challenge and became a Cadet
There is one indisputable and time-proven fact:
Whenever one faced a personal or spiritual trial
Chaplain Camp could be counted on to compassionately act.
He was one of us as much as he could be
Adventurously riding his "bike," yet always divine.
In his robe or holding the sticks
Dedicated and loyal to the Long Gray Line.
Another chapter is drawing to an honorable close

In the book of Chaplain Camp's wonderful life.
One that was written I'm sure he will attest
With the help of a strong, supportive, and loving wife.
With Cadets at West Point of all races and creeds
He established a permanent unbreakable bond.
In sincerity and truth serving the Lord and the Corps
Chaplain Camp performed his duties "Above and Beyond!"

Dan's Norwin Athletic Hall of Fame acceptance speech in 2018

Norwin has a proud athletic history, and I am honored to be a part of that tradition. I am proud this evening to be honored with my fellow inductees. I am grateful to Mr. Tom Shirley and the Hall of Fame Committee for selecting me for this honor and to Dan Cowell for initially recommending me. I wouldn't be standing here tonight if it wasn't for my school administrators, teachers, classmates, and teammates who I am so grateful for. I am thankful for having played for head coach John Yaccino and assistant coach Al Lynn.

As we know, the game of football requires discipline, hard work, and teamwork. My mom and dad instilled these qualities in me when I was young and throughout our family life. Norwin football and Coach Yaccino enhanced these qualities that helped me prepare for my challenges at West Point, Ranger School, and for the accomplishments I was blessed with. I went from a Norwin Knight to become an Army Black Knight where I learned to live and cherish the West Point motto of Duty-Honor-County.

Most of all, I am grateful to my mom and dad for instilling in me a Christian upbringing. When a life-changing adversity came into my life, the Biblical verse Philippians 4:13, "I can do all things through Christ who strengthens me" became the cornerstone of my faith that sustains me.

In closing, thank you for your prayers and support of my family and me. Thank you for being here tonight, and thank you, Norwin High School, for bestowing me this honor. I am proud to be a Norwin Knight. May God's blessings be with all of you.

Norwin Athletic Hall of Fame member Darryl Bertani on Dan's selection for the high school's Hall of Fame

C ourage can be exhibited in a variety of ways. Obviously, it is found on a battlefield, and it is also on display in sports and everyday life. No matter where it occurs, courage has one common denominator and that is adversity. Trying to overcome hardship requires special recognition.

Dan Priatko has been dealt one of life's cruelest fates having become permanently disabled through a horrific accident. Yet, he has never given up and never will. He has stared misfortune in the eye, but he will never let it overcome him or define him. He is a fighter teeming with willpower and determination, which serves him well in his daily endeavors. He is a prime example of someone who doesn't surrender despite the odds against him. For these reasons and for being a stellar athlete, scholar, and person, Dan Priatko is entering the Norwin Athletic Hall of Fame for which he is "honored and grateful."

A 1980 graduate, Priatko gained distinction both on the football field and in the classroom at Norwin. Playing three years, he stood out on the gridiron as a running back and linebacker. He was named a team captain and selected Most Valuable Player by his coaches and teammates his senior season. Off the field he was more distinguished. An 'A' student, Priatko was voted Senior Class President. Highlighting his laurels was being chosen as Norwin's Most Outstanding Male Student by the principal, faculty, and students.

With an eye toward a military career like his brother, Lt. Colonel David, Priatko received an appointment to West Point where he played football for four years. He again excelled in academics, becoming a Battalion Commander, one of twelve such Cadet leadership positions. In addition, he won the coveted award for having the highest GPA of a senior varsity letterman. A 1984 graduate, he completed both Airborne and Ranger schools.

Tragedy struck in March of 1985. Dan, son of ex-Steeler Bill Priatko, was involved in a life-changing accident that left him severely injured. Hospitalized for a year and a half, he overcame medical odds and was released. Despite his disabilities and long hours of strenuous rehabilitation, he worked as a recreational aide at care centers, currently volunteering at Redstone Highlands. He has aided Norwin football teams with encouraging pre-game speeches.

Dan is a solid Hall of Fame inspiration and a very positive influence for athletes and mankind. His strength of heart, refusal to relinquish hope, and proclivity for helping others make Dan Priatko a champion for all of us and for all time.

Dan's Norwin High School Distinguished Alumni Award acceptance speech in 2018

I congratulate my fellow inductees and I am honored to be here with them.

For me to receive this honor, it has to be shared with those who are the biggest reason for any of my success and accomplishments: my mom and dad, my brother and sisters, relatives and friends who have supported me and helped me over the years. So many of you are here this evening, and I am so grateful for all of you.

To my teachers, administrators, staff, classmates, football coaches, and teammates at Norwin High School, thank you so much. To my parish priest, Father Igor Soroka of St. Nicholas Orthodox Church in Donora, who has been a great influence on my church and spiritual life with his love, guidance, and compassion. Father Igor is here this evening. Thank you, Father Igor.

Most of all, I thank my Lord and Savior, Jesus Christ, who gives me hope and strength. Every day, I try to remember the words in my Bible when Paul in Philippians says, "I am content to be in whatever circumstance I am in." I have faith that when I get to heaven, I will have a new body.

In closing, I say to you what I said when speaking to a group of Sunday school students at their CCD at St. Stephen's Byzantine Catholic Church, here in my hometown of North Huntingdon. They were Norwin High School seniors, about forty of them. After my talk, a girl in the class asked me, "Doesn't it bother you to know that you had such a promising career ahead of you and this happened to you?" I said to her and the class, "If anything I have said to you brings just one of you closer to Jesus, I am glad that my accident happened."

Thank you all for being here this evening to bring joy to my fellow inductees and me. God bless you.

About the Author

S cott Brown has written eight other books and is working on a book about University of Kentucky basketball pioneer Reggie Warford. Brown covered the Pittsburgh Steelers from 2006-2014 for ESPN and *The Pittsburgh Tribune-Review*. He also covered Penn State football for the *Tribune-Review*. Brown previously worked at *Florida Today* and *The Philadelphia Inquirer*. A Greensburg, Pennsylvania, resident, Brown can be reached at scott_brown00@yahoo.com. Follow him on Twitter at @ ScottBrown_15.

His previous books are:
- *Hope & Heartbreak: Beyond The Numbers of the Opioid Epidemic*
- *In The Locker Room With Tunch Ilkin*
- *Pittsburgh Steelers Fans' Bucket List*
- *Heaven Sent: The Heather Miller Story* (co-author Wendy Miller)
- *What It Means To Be A Nittany Lion* (co-author Lou Prato)
- *Miracle in the Making: The Adam Taliaferro Story* (co-author Sam Carchidi)
- *King of the Mount: The Jim Phelan Story*
- *Lions Kings: One of the Greatest Offenses in College Football History*

CPSIA information can be obtained
at www.ICGtesting.com
Printed in the USA
LVHW010754240321
682049LV00011B/65